Forming a Partnership

And Making It Work

Ira Nottonson

Entrepreneur
MAGAZINE'S

LEGAL GUIDE

Forming a Partnership

And Making It Work

Ep
Entrepreneur.
Press

Editorial director: Jere L. Calmes
Cover design: Desktop Miracles, Inc.
Composition and production: Eliot House Productions

This publication is designed to provide accurate and authoritative information in regard to
the subject matter covered. It is sold with the understanding that the publisher is not engaged
in rendering legal, accounting, or other professional services. If legal advice or other expert
assistance is required, the services of a competent professional person should be sought.

Scales ©Rzymu

Library of Congress Cataloging-in-Publication Data
Nottonson, Ira N., 1933–
Forming a partnership: and making it work/by Ira Nottonson.
  p.   cm.
ISBN-13: 978-1-59918-071-7 (alk. paper)
ISBN-10: 1-59918-071-5 (alk. paper)
1. Partnership—United States—Popular works. I. Title.
KF1375.Z9N68 2007
346.73'0682—dc22   2006100476

Printed in Canada

12 11 10 09 08 07   10 9 8 7 6 5 4 3 2 1

Contents

PART ONE
The Partnership
Formation and Implications of the Legal Partnership

CHAPTER 1
A Simple Analysis of Partnership:

v

CHAPTER 2

Developing Your Partnership **15**

PART TWO

The Partnership Relationships

All the Relationships Involved in Surviving and Succeeding in
the Modern Business Community

CHAPTER 3

You Can't Do It All Yourself **23**

CHAPTER 4

Business, Family, and Partnership **31**

CHAPTER 16

Putting It in Writing **147**

CHAPTER 17

Being Deceived by Your Partner: Why Trust Is So Important **157**

CHAPTER 18

Parents as Partners: The Good, the Bad, and the Ugly **165**

Preface

The question of partnerships really involves just about every working relationship in a for-profit business enterprise. It is for this reason that many collateral relationships have been included in this work. The salesperson who has a personal knowledge of and a close working relationship with your client base is a partner of sorts, whether you like it or not. He or she deserves the respect of management and the partners. Remember, the partner can't really leave and take clients or customers from the business. There is, however, no similar restraint on employees. The implicit partnership of a spouse or significant other always calls for some consideration. And don't forget the lender who, although not a technical partner, often controls the purse strings. This book addresses those collateral relationships because they are the core elements of a functioning partnership business.

A significant problem that this book is designed to address is that most books are predicated on the technical aspects of "how to." The problem of how to is easily enough solved because there are a myriad of technical writings that explain how to do just about everything. The real question should not be how to. It should be "should I?" Although it might be possible to create a list of all the things an entrepreneur should or should not do, the reality is that rarely does anyone follow the guidelines of a list. The real-life situations that have generated success or failure in business are the examples that create a reality for the reader. This book is designed to achieve this all-important element missing on the current business bookshelf.

Another problem I find in most business books is that optimism far outweighs the pessimism concerning just about every business subject. When the negative side of a question is examined, it usually receives short shrift. To be sure, the positive suggests success and the negative suggests otherwise. On the other hand, it is appropriate, if not mandatory, that the reader, the entrepreneur, be given an even hand in order to make his or her best decisions. This book tries to more evenly examine the potentials of every subject. If it appears to be heavily accented on the negative in any chapter, it is because the realities of the marketplace have suggested that the reader be properly informed. I make no apology for having erred on the side of being conservative. The realities of the marketplace offer the best examples of what to do, how to do it, and when. Even the examples found in most chapters will be designed to show what not to do or the best way to avoid a problem or the way in which any businessperson can get lost in a conundrum by virtue of not understanding a basic precept of business. Chapter 18 "Parents as Partners" is a perfect example of this. And no apology is in order.

The last comment on this book in general is for the reader to understand the reason for redundancy. Since each chapter is designed to examine partnerships from a slightly different perspective, you will find that the same conundrum appears in various chapters in a slightly different context. It is important that you get a look at these problems from different vantage points.

How to Use this Book

Whatever business you may be in or expect to be in, this book is designed to help you understand the business relationships necessary for survival and success. It is not a how-to book in the usual sense. It is, however, a how-to book in a somewhat unique sense. It is designed to explain how to deal with, how to cope with, and how to negotiate with the myriad of people and businesses so necessary to maintain the continuity of your business.

The Concept of Partnership

The concept of partnership in its singular sense is important to those of you who choose to share the obligations and prerogatives of your business with someone else. The concept of partnership in its plural sense is equally important, to understand the relationships that you did not choose but that are relevant to your everyday business activity.

The more subtle aspects of partnership are represented by the relationship of the participants in every business organization, whether it's called a partnership, a corporation, or a limited liability company. These other legal entities also involve the partnership concept, because the questions of investment, profits, taxes, and personal liability are essentially the same.

Thinking that these explanations complete the partnership discussion is, however, entirely wrong. The concept goes much further. The relationship with an investor in a company is certainly within the category of a legal partnership because, by owning a piece of the company, the investor is an actual partner—albeit, in many cases, an inactive one. Yet, the responsibility of a company to its lender, who normally does not own a piece of the company, is every bit as important, if not more so. After all, an equity partner can't really pull the rug out from under a failing company. A lender can! This, then, leads to the idea of following all relationships on which a business depends for its success, including its very survival, even though the legal aspect of the relationship is not designated as a partnership per se.

This book is designed to ensure that this practical side of operating a business is not lost in the legal jargon so often the province of business books. This is accomplished by examining all types of partnership relationships as they pertain to the small-business community. The idea is to help the small business owner avoid each problem before it becomes necessary to repair it. This book stands on the front lines of business as a reality check to augment the technical legal aspects of partnerships.

Worksheets, etc.

Each chapter is a continuous journey along that road to understanding. You will find short stories, which introduce each chapter. There is no better way to understand the foibles of the human animal than to ruminate about the realities of actual events. You will also find legal approaches to some of the more convoluted situations. These are not designed to replace good legal or accounting advice but should give you basic understanding of the problem.

At the close of each chapter, you will find a worksheet that should cause you to further examine, from your own perspective, the lessons and attitudes revealed in that chapter.

Use of the CD

Redundancy is not a bad word. The entire concept of a mantra (an incantation) is the predicate for most disciplines. This repetition—in business, religion, or other organizational efforts—is not unusual. Even the logo of Nike® is a part of this discipline: "Just do it!" In the context of business, both profits and nonprofits, the concept is usually embodied in a mission statement. It may not be the words that each employee or that management repeats every hour, but it certainly has its place in the discipline of the business.

This book is based on a mantra: "Failure is not a way of life. It is a moment in time. Get over it and move on!" Going on a trip, business or social, might not suggest taking this book with you. But making copies of the sidebars for all chapters, together with the worksheets from each chapter, should keep you on the "straight and narrow" as you take a peek at one or the other periodically.

Try out the concepts and be the best you can be at what you do and what you want to accomplish.

❑ ❑ ❑✗

A big thank you is in order to Jere Calmes of Entrepreneur Press, whose idea about beginning each chapter with a short story made the book more readable. A second big thank you is in order to Karen Billipp of Eliot House Productions, without whose encouragement and critical analysis this book might not have become a reality.

PART ONE

The Partnership

Formation and Implications of the Legal Partnership

CHAPTER 1

A Simple
Analysis of
Partnership
Compared to Other Legal Entities

The Challenge of Partnership
A Story about How It Happens

Scott and Harold had been friends for years. As so often is the case, they both decided that this relationship represented a solid basis for a business partnership. Unfortunately, their trust in each other in terms of picking up checks at restaurants and buying tickets to sporting events, led them to create a very casual partnership. It was essentially a handshake. Although this is indeed enough to constitute a legal partnership, it lacked any of the essential ingredients that would protect each of them from the vulnerabilities of business as well as from each other. As time went on, Scott, being somewhat more conservative than his partner, bought a pickup for the business and used it as his family car as well. Harold, being somewhat more flamboyant than Scott, decided to buy a $60,000 luxury car. The cars were, of course, both bought in the name of the business. The rationale of Harold's purchase was that he was the salesperson and needed the car to make the appropriate impression on customers. Without getting confirmation from his partner, Harold also bought a boat, a condo in the mountains, and ski-lift tickets for the entire season at two resorts. His rationale was the same: these were amenities that a salesperson needed to salt the mine and make the right impression on customers. It wasn't long before Harold grew tired of the traveling and frustrated with the slow growth of the business; in fact, Harold, who had money of his own, decided that working was a bad habit that he'd like to put in his past. He left the company and agreed to forfeit any interest in the company to Scott.

However, this hardly turned out to be a good turn for Scott because, in terms of basic partnership law, the general partnership, which was what Scott and Harold had created, is subject to joint and several liability. This means that each partner is completely obliged to pay all partnership obligations, whether incurred by himself or by his partner. This is true as long as the "appearance" of the purchase is deemed to be for partnership purposes. After Harold left for Europe, the bills started coming into the business. Scott began to realize that his high-living partner had gone a little over the top in representing the company, the partnership. Scott was now responsible for all debts on the car, the condo, the boat, and the ski-lift tickets. Although it is true that Scott may be able to get partial reimbursement from Harold on a legal basis, as a practical matter, this solution is untenable. While each partner owes a fiduciary duty to the other, a duty of trust to act in the best interests of the company, it would be difficult to prove that Harold acted contrary to the best interests of the business.

❏ ❏ ❏

- Do you think a partnership agreement in writing might have precluded this problem?
- Don't you think that "substantial purchases" should require more than one signature to bind the company?
- Do you think a corporation or a limited liability company could have avoided this situation?
- Do you think limited liability should be high on the priority list of a new partnership?

The Prerogatives and Obligations of Operating a Business

Operating a business is the terminology used for creating a profit by selling products or services. In its simplest form, a business is operated by a single person and is called a "sole proprietorship." The next kind of legal entity under which the business can be operated is called a "partnership." It is the operation of a business by two or more people. And in this context, the word "partnership" can also stand for corporations, limited liability companies, or any other legal entities. The idea is to take time, raw material, component parts, or finished product(s) and sell them to a consumer at a profit.

Determining the Profit

This profit is determined by deducting from the sales price all expenses necessary to create the sales. These expenses include costs of the product or costs necessary to produce the service or the product and all other costs of operating the business, often referred to as Salaries and General Administrative expenses or SG&A. Although having a variety of definitions, SG&A represents all the expenses, aside from costs of product, that are necessary to operate the business. These include rent, employee salaries, telephone, electricity, transportation; and, just about everything that usually needs to be paid monthly, whether the business is successful or not.

Before You Can Spend the Profit

Aside from the various taxes that the business must pay for the privilege of doing business within a particular state, and the taxes that must be deducted for the various federal obligations such as social security and Medicare, the owner or owners must pay income tax on the profit they derive from the business. Because of this, the government is sometimes referred to, tongue in cheek, as another partner in the business.

Putting the Sole Proprietorship and the Partnership in the Same Box

The reason for lumping together the concepts of sole proprietorship and partnership is that the advantage of the pass-through tax privilege and the disadvantage of the lack of limited liability protection are similar in both cases. Although there are other legal entities that share these concepts to some extent, the concepts are most clear when comparing these two.

Sole Proprietorship and General Partnership

When you're deciding under what legal entity your company should do business, don't let anyone confuse you. If you've decided to start a business by yourself, from your home or otherwise, you don't really need to use any particular legal form, such as a corporation or a limited partnership. You merely have to file (in most cases) a d/b/a, "doing business as." If your name is Charles Brown and you want your company name to be CB Mfg. Co., you will file a d/b/a with your local municipal authority. It will say "Charles Brown d/b/a (doing business as) CB Mfg. Co." This will allow people who have a business relationship with CB Mfg. Co. to find out who the true owner is. They are entitled to know this. This lays the foundation of the relationship between you, your business, and your business community. If you are in business for yourself, your business entity is simply referred to as a *sole proprietorship*.

If you do business with one or more partners, and merely file a d/b/a with their names doing business as the name of your company, you are operating a *simple partnership*: Charles Brown and Alice Faye d/b/a CB Mfg.Co.

Joint and Several Liability

The problem with a sole proprietorship or a simple partnership, also called a general partnership, is that the owner or owners are responsible for all financial obligations of the company. If one partner signs a contract, all the partners are responsible. This is called *joint and several liability*. It means that any one partner can be sued for the entire obligation even if he or she is only a 10 percent partner; even if he or she never signed the contract; even if he or she didn't even know about the contract. This is also true if someone sues the company for a tortious act (a tort)—such as slipping on a banana peel that someone negligently left lying on the floor in a store.

> Don't ever lose sight of the joint and several liability aspect of day-to-day operations.

In the case of a contract, the vendor who sues the company need not be concerned about this "insider" distribution of responsibility. The outsider can sue any partner he or she chooses or may sue all the partners at the same time and, if the judgment is rendered against all the partners, the outsider can actually choose the partner from whom he or she wants to collect the judgment. The partner who was not actually involved in the particular business circumstance that led to the litigation and who can show that he or she is not responsible for the judgment, may then sue the responsible partner for reimbursement. This reimbursement, however, may be long after the noninvolved partner has paid the judgment to the outsider. Remember the Scott and Harold situation.

Corporation

The problem of liability led to the creation of a legal entity called a corporation. By forming a corporation, none of the individual owners, or shareholders, is liable to an outsider except under certain unique circumstances such as fraud or misrepresentation. Such a situation allows the outsider to "pierce the corporate veil"—in other words, to break the protective shield of the corporation. Aside from these types of situations, however, the corporate shield will afford the owners, the shareholders, adequate protection from liability stemming from normal business activities of the corporation.

The Corporate Signature

Keep in mind, however, that the owners must sign all contracts with their respective "corporate signature" in order to maintain this protective shield. They must sign as corporate officers; for example, Charles Brown, Vice President. If he merely signs as Charles Brown, he is not taking advantage of the corporate protection and is acknowledging that Charles Brown, *individual* will be responsible for the corporate debt.

> The corporation can give you certain protections but it is not designed to cover all contingencies.

Why would a corporate officer do this? Some do it because they don't understand the difference. Some do it because many

> Be sure you sign all corporate documents with your corporate signature.

vendors and lessors will not accept a bare corporate signature. For example, in the case of a very substantial purchase or lease, the vendor or lessor may feel that the corporation's assets are not strong enough to represent solid security for the purchase. Closely held corporations and new corporations usually have just enough working capital to maintain continuity of the business. Also, most such corporations, especially new ones, don't have a lot of equity in their existing assets. Most of their assets are either on long-term lease, or have been purchased with borrowed money, and have likely been pledged as security for the loan.

The Security Interest

In either case, the lessor or lender, having taken a down payment, will likely have taken a security interest in the assets to protect against the failure of the lessee or borrower to make the payments on the balance of the purchase price. In the event that the payments are not made in accordance with the terms of such a contract or lease, the goods (if not already sold) or the equipment can be repossessed by the vendor or lessor by virtue of the security interest properly recorded.

The seller or lessor of new goods or equipment, as well as anyone lending money, recognizes that he or she cannot rely on the assets of the corporation to collect monies owed because these assets usually serve as security for the original purchase or lease. In such a case, these new vendors will certainly insist on a separate individual signature as a guarantee. In fact, it is likely that even the original purveyors of goods or equipment have insisted on personal signatures guaranteeing the payment in addition to the security interest they took.

The Guaranty Signature

This is the reason you will sometimes see two signatures on a document. One will be *Charles Brown, Vice President* and the second will be *Charles Brown*. This makes Charles Brown, the individual, just as liable for the debt as the corporation, which was bound to the contract by the Charles Brown, Vice President, signature. This should suggest to you that the corporate shield is only a limited protection, hinging on the concept of joint and several liability allowing the creditor to seek the entire balance owed from either the corporation or the individual, or both.

Subchapter S Corporation

Tax laws impose taxes on some corporations as if they were separate people, which, by law, the corporation actually is. This is called a C corporation. This tax situation differentiates it from an S corporation, also known as a subchapter S corporation. An S corporation, unlike the C, will be taxed as if it were a general partnership, with each partner being taxed for a percentage of the corporation's profits on each of their individual tax returns: the pass-through concept. The disadvantage of an S corporation from a tax standpoint is that the individuals will be taxed on the profits of the business as their personal income . . . whether they actually received the profits or not.

The disadvantage of the C corporation, from a tax standpoint, is that there is a potential for a double tax. The corporation will pay a tax first on the corporate profits, whereupon the shareholders, to whom the profits are distributed as corporate dividends, will pay a second tax on an individual basis. There are reasons for this apparently inappropriate double tax but they will not be taken up here. There are also methods by which a closely held corporation can avoid such a double taxation by increasing salaries and bonuses, providing these increases are cautiously maintained within reasonable limits. Keep in mind, however, that each corporate entity has its own advantages and disadvantages. Be sure you speak to your professional financial advisor before making a decision as to which one to use.

Board of Directors

Both types of corporations function with a board of directors, elected by the shareholders. The members of the board of directors may or may not be shareholders. In most small, closely-held corporations, they usually are shareholders.

Very often, it is a family relationship. In larger corporations, the shareholders often choose to have a board of directors composed of people who are not shareholders. Many think that this kind of group will give them greater objectivity in helping management make business decisions.

Sometimes an individual might be invited to become a member of a board because of the particular influence which he or she may have in the business or banking community and which might be considered helpful to the company's growth. Financial people are often asked to join when management is considering the possibility of borrowing substantial sums of money, or making a public offering.

> Your board of directors can serve a variety of purposes.

Shareholders' liability is limited to the amount of their actual investment in the company unless they have personally guaranteed a corporate debt. Members of the board of directors have no liability to business creditors except, of course, in the event that they are guilty of fraud or misrepresentation. Notwithstanding this lack of responsibility for normal business decisions, they are not immune to having lawsuits brought against them, whether such litigation is legitimate or frivolous. Serving on a board of directors has this potential for annoyance, if not responsibility. It is for this reason that many people who serve on boards will insist on having the company take out directors and officers liability insurance on their behalf. Keep in mind that even this umbrella protection will not protect either management or members of the board from liability as the result of fraud or misrepresentation. The shareholders who are not participating in business decisions are only liable to the extent of their actual investment in the company.

Other Insurance Coverage

Consider too that whether you are a sole proprietor or a general partner in a simple partnership, a corporation, or any other legal entity, you will always want to maintain appropriate insurance coverage for things over which you have no control. There are many times when a corporation may be sued on the basis of something having nothing to do with the business's purpose. If a customer trips on a foreign object left on the floor of the retail premises, regardless of who might have been responsible for putting it there, he or she may sue the company for negligence. If a customer is having a meal and gets sick, he or she may sue the company. This kind of collateral responsibility should always be covered by liability insurance designed to handle just such a contingency.

Limited Partnership

There are many variations that call for a particular legal entity to be used in any given circumstance. Each has its reason, usually because of the investors involved. For example, some investors want the protection of a corporation but want one or more persons to be financially responsible, given that most of the activity will be under that person's singular discretion. For this purpose, they may form a *limited partnership* where the general partner will be totally responsible for any loss that the partnership suffers, and the limited partners, just as the shareholders in a corporation, will be responsible only for the amount of their investment in the partnership.

The limited partners must be careful, however, because under this format, they are not allowed to participate in the actual operation of the partnership business. If they do, they can forfeit their limited partner protection and end up being treated by outsiders as just general partners. You will remember the joint and several liability that applies to general partners! Note the story about Roger at the beginning of Chapter 2.

Limited Liability Company

This liability problem then led to a limited liability company in which the limited partners have no personal liability aside from their actual investment in the company, even though they are allowed to participate in the operation of the company. Keep in mind that, whatever legal entity you use, you must always be conscious not only of the liability issue but of tax implications as well.

Family Limited Liability Company

The last variation of real consequence is the relatively new family limited liability company, which is limited to a family relationship and has, as its core investments, only family assets. This entity is particularly useful in instances of family succession of a business as it allows periodic transfer of stock with limited tax implications. If you have a family transition situation, you might want to examine the extent to which this is available in your particular state. Keep in mind that there are many insurance programs that can aid in such a transition, ameliorating many otherwise onerous tax implications. With regard to other, nonfamily transitions, you might want to examine the use of 401K plans, sweat equity programs, and the like. Be sure to see your professional to ensure that any such transition is handled properly.

Short- and Long-Term Goals

Many purposes are served in the creation of a business. Each goal should be carefully analyzed before making a judgment about the particular legal entity to be used. The people who put up the capital to create the business will normally have the greatest influence on this decision. The nature of the business and whether their investment is for short- or long-term purposes, will dictate, to a great degree, the kind of format they will suggest.

In one case, the entrepreneur will see the operation of the business as a final goal, an instrument by which to feed the family and ultimately convert the earned equity of the business to a retirement income. In such a case, the particular legal format to be used may be of lesser importance. In another case, the group raising capital for the formation of the business may aspire to having the business acquired by a bigger company or to converting the business concept into a franchise operation, or perhaps entertain the singular goal of taking the company public. These are some of the many goals that will cause investors to think carefully about the legal format they will initially choose.

> Make sure you understand the short- and long-term goals of the business early on.

Other Classes of Stock

Some long-term goals of the investors might also include their ability to avoid certain onerous tax implications, including the "recapture" of tax savings accumulated during an early business period, or the ease with which one entity may be converted to another. This may lead to an even more sophisticated situation where more than one class of stock is issued, and where options are attached to stock certificates, where certain classes of stock have certain prerogatives not given to the others. As these purposes become increasingly evident, your best advice should be sought from your professionals to ensure that you make the correct decisions both for the short- and the long-term goals of the company. And be sure to seek this advice early on!

Worksheet Questions

1. What can cause you to be personally liable in addition to your personal signature?

2. What is the advantage of the limited partnership concept to you as an investor?

3. What do you need to be careful about as a limited partner?

4. What is the advantage to a subchapter S corporation?

5. What is the disadvantage to a C corporation?

Developing Your Partnership

The Limited Partnership Problem

Roger had put together a limited partnership to raise sufficient capital to buy a franchise operation of 12 retail stores. The investors had great faith in him because he had previously been executive vice president of the franchise company. This experience gave great comfort to the group of franchisees who were investing in the company. One problem was that the franchisees were located in different parts of the country and would not be able to participate in the operating of the business. A limited partnership was perfect for this relationship given that the general partner (Roger) would be completely responsible for all obligations of the business, and the limited partners would have only their original investments at risk . . . nothing more. So long as the franchisees did not participate in the operation of the business, their liability was limited to that extent.

For a variety of reasons, including the national economy during the period after the purchase, the business began to fail. All the limited partners came to the city to discuss the matter with Roger. He was accused of failing to operate the company properly and the discussion led to the preliminary decision that the operation of the business should be taken over by the limited partners. The limited partners, however, faced a conundrum. It was pointed out to them that if they took over management, they would lose their limited liability and automatically fall into the category of a general partnership instead of a limited partnership. This would allow all creditors to bring legal actions against each and every one of them. Their alternative would be to merely let Roger continue to operate the business with the likely scenario that they would all lose their original investments. They decided that losing their original investments was a better course of action than making themselves vulnerable to lawsuits for all the money that the limited partnership owed.

❑ ❑ ❑

• Do you think that forming a limited liability company or a corporation would have better protected these limited partners? Would this choice have given them the prerogative of taking over management without making them vulnerable to lawsuits?

It is a fact of life: engines do not run without fuel and businesses do not function without money. The questions of investment and lending become high priorities in the world of business. Whether the business is operated as a sole proprietorship, a partnership, a corporation, or a limited liability company, you can be sure that questions of investment, return of investment, return on investment, limitations on liability, and the tax implications of profit are always in the minds of the owners.

About Limited Liability

It should be clear that your choice of a legal entity through which to develop your business is a decision to be made carefully. In Chapter 1, you saw one partner subjected to the irresponsibility of the other. Remember Scott and Harold? But also remember that time and circumstance change the effect of the partnership relationship in many ways. If Scott and Harold had built a very successful business, Harold's expenditures might have been more appropriate. After all, successful selling involves creating the appearance of success. Many of Harold's expenditures served to build that facade.

Even if Scott and Harold had created a limited liability company or a corporation to protect the partners from joint and several liability, the business would have been responsible for the obligations anyway. The relationship of Scott and Harold as equal partners created a situation in which people outside the company could assume that Harold had the authority to act on behalf of the business and was authorized to incur the obligations that he did.

Being Too Smart by Half

In the above example, you saw that investors in Roger's business thought they were protecting their investments by creating a limited partnership. The problem was that, in a critical time in the history of the business, they were prevented from taking over management of the company when new management might have saved the day. The downside risk, however, of being responsible for the company's debts, dictated against this decision. Remember too that these limited partners were all from out of town.

> In a general partnership, your partners can create liability for you even if they incur debts or obligations without consulting with you.

The Concept of Taxation

As you've noted, the pass-through concept of taxation certainly suggests that, in a closely held corporation, you avoid creating a C corporation. However, looking at the practical side of this question, we find an alternative approach. Keep in mind that, as your business grows, you will likely increase your management salaries commensurate with that growth. This will leave the company with no profit on which to pay taxes. Even after you've reached a reasonable salary level, there are still ways to increase your compensation package by bonuses and amenities not available to you in the early days of the business. There are, of course, limitations to the amount of compensation that management can and should take from the company. The caution is to be careful and seek professional advice. Overstepping in this area can generate back taxes, interest, and penalties.

The other side of this coin is that you would have to go "way over the top" to violate this concept in the small-business marketplace. Still, it is this double taxation that dictates against the formation of the C corporation in most cases, because the limited liability company, as well as the subchapter S corporation, accomplish the basic purpose of limiting liability without getting involved in the tax problem. Remember that these entities as well as most partnerships enjoy the advantage of the pass-through tax benefit. The entity is not taxed on its profit; the individuals are taxed on the profits on their personal income, which includes the profits or the dividends distributed to them. For the more sophisticated business that expects dramatic profits and for other purposes, the C corporation can be the right entity to choose. Be sure you discuss this with your professional advisor.

The Bottom Line

There are two things that the reader should understand about partnership protection. The first is that *general partnerships are not recommended for the long term.* Although the simplicity of their formation (by a mere handshake or a previous relationship) makes them easy to get started, it should be clear that the vulnerability of each partner to the other as well as to the general business community does not recommend the general partnership as a preferable business entity for the long term.

Negative aspects of the general partnership should be carefully considered:

- Partners are as responsible for company obligations as they are entitled to profits.
- Outsiders are not likely to find comfort in investing in a general partnership.
- Partners may legally bind each other without the other's consent.
- There is joint and several liability among partners, as well as liability for the wrongdoings of other partners.

- There is no limited liability protection for the debts of the business.
- There are restrictions on the transferability of partnership interests.

The Partnership Relationship

The partnership relationship is embodied in all the other legal entities as well, even though they may be called limited liability companies or corporations, limited partnerships, or even the most sophisticated of partnerships such as the family limited liability company. All involve the relationship between people who are investors or managers of the business. All participants are interested in protecting their personal assets from vulnerability to other partners or to the business community as a whole. The best way to protect yourself, in any of the legal entities you may choose to use, is to create an agreement that spells out the obligations and prerogatives of the parties.

> Don't forget the advantage of creating a legal entity that affords you limited liability protection.

The Agreement

If you create a corporation, you will have a set of bylaws spelling out the rights that management and investors have in the company. In a limited liability company, these same rights are detailed in an operating agreement. In a partnership, the agreement is referred to as a partnership agreement. Although it is not likely to include every conceivable problem that could arise, there are certain basics to which the parties should direct their attention. It is very much like creating a business plan to the extent that it serves as a road map for the future of the people involved in the business.

- Each party has certain obligations, and these should be spelled out.
- Each party is entitled to a percentage of the profit and, in most cases, is not responsible for any loss incurred in the business (except in the case of a general partnership).
- Although a party may choose to sell his interest in the business, the other parties should have the first right-of-purchase to avoid having a stranger enter the business.

- Bringing new parties into the business may dilute the interests of the original parties and should be examined to determine what the protocol should be.
- There should always be a method by which disagreements can be resolved without the need for litigation.
- There should be a periodic valuation done of the business in order to create a value for each person's interest should they decide to exit the company.
- There should be an initial agreement as to the short- and long-term goals of the business so that all investors and participants are of the same mind.
- There should be some agreement as to when profits will be reinvested or distributed to the investors.
- There should be a decision about the extent to which management can make decisions and spend money without obtaining permission of the investors.

As you can see, the number of conditions and considerations are nearly endless. Just keep in mind that, if you want to avoid problems, your best course is to understand and acknowledge what they are and to prepare alternatives for their resolution . . . before they occur.

There is an adage among lawyers regarding successful limited partnerships. "At the beginning of a limited partnership, the general partner has the experience and the limited partners have the money. At the end of a limited partnership, the general partner has the money and the limited partners have the experience." Can you see how this juxtaposition of experience and money works?

PART TWO

The Partnership Relationships

All the Relationships Involved in Surviving and Succeeding in the Modern Business Community

You Can't Do It All Yourself

Don't Tell Me What I Already Know

Lisa left college shortly after her third year was completed. She had studied business management and wanted to move ahead by going into business for herself. Her intention was to finish her schooling by taking business classes at night. She took over a printing business that was doing very badly. In fact, the business was essentially on the road to bankruptcy. Lisa and her partner Josephine jumped in with both feet.

They hired a printer after being in business for a while. Lisa had been doing the printing to familiarize herself with the equipment, its capabilities, and shortcomings. This new printer gave Lisa an opportunity to make outside sales calls while the printer produced the product and Josephine handled the counter.

My Experience and Yours

One day after sales calls, Lisa returned to the shop and found that the printer had not finished a job on the press. When asked about this, the printer replied, "This is a four-hour job. That's why it's not finished." Lisa's response was immediate! "You're fired! I've operated that press for only a few months but I would have finished this job in one-and-a-half hours."

The End Game

Knowing the capability of your equipment is a necessary part of your education in many businesses. The end of the story is threefold. The printer apologized and was rehired by Lisa to work with her for the next four years. Lisa and Josephine, as partners, rebuilt the business and sold it at a substantial profit. Lisa finished her education and earned her degree in business.

- Do you think it's possible to know the particulars of everybody's job in your business?
- Do you want to hire people who are as good as you at a particular job . . . or better than you?
- Which are the most important aspects of your business that you should learn?

Being the Coach of the Team

Although you don't have to be able to operate each piece of machinery in a service business, you should understand the nature of the equipment, its capabilities, its shortcomings, and its production capacity in terms of time and product. If you don't have a handle on these aspects, you won't know what to expect of the people who are using the equipment. You might not want to be a salesperson but you should certainly go on sales calls with your salespeople to understand the nature of the best presentations as well as the questions and responses necessary to make a sale. Being a coach doesn't mean that you need to play all the positions on the team. It does mean that you need to know the responsibilities of each player in order for the team to function properly.

Cross-Training

In most businesses, there is a person to perform each necessary function. What happens when that person is absent? You cannot allow the business to falter or fail. You must make arrangements for that job function to be taken over, even if only for a temporary period, in order to maintain continuity of the business. The best way to ensure that the transitions will be seamless is to make sure that others can assume those responsibilities. Many employees don't like the cross-training concept because they feel less important to the business if they know that someone else is capable of delivering that service. On the other hand, each employee must recognize that the business and its ability to endure is the key and the higher priority. Care must be taken to ensure that this delicate balance is maintained.

Make sure you understand each person's responsibilities before you build your business team.

The Virtual Office and Outsourcing

There are some businesses that can be operated by a single individual without any actual team of employees. After all, if you go into business, it is usually a good idea not to try to attempt to function at every level. This all-encompassing approach to business can be inimical to the best interests of the business, especially at the early stages of development. You should do all the things that you and your team are capable of doing without trying to do those things that you can't do. If you are manufacturing a product, you might want to use a professional distribution system instead of trying to develop your own. If you want to get product into the marketplace in the most expeditious, cost-effective manner, you might want to retain the services of a good advertising agency instead of trying to learn and implement systems with which you are unfamiliar.

People who have started businesses by themselves know that, from the very first idea (sometimes conceived by waking up at 3:00 A.M.), initiating a business predicated on that idea is no easy task. It takes a variety of intellectual and emotional strengths as well as focus, foresight, and discipline. The first question the entrepreneur ought to ask is: Do I have all the intellectual and emotional tools to build this business? Looking in the mirror to find the answer to this question is a difficult emotional task. Accepting the fact that you might have some of the tools and not all the tools is the honest answer. Finding people whose abilities can complement your own is often a good idea.

The Bare Beginning of the Game

It must be noted at the outset of any business venture that the idea, by itself, is only the bare beginning of the game. According to an American friend living in the United Kingdom, the people there are very creative. Within one hour in a pub, a group of people can literally come up with a bunch of really good ideas. The problem is that, when everyone goes home, the ideas are usually left at the bar. It is the implementation of an idea that creates the venture, not the idea by itself. The reality that reflects this finding is that some creative people think that their idea should entitle them to a percentage of ownership in any business that ensues from the idea. Although there are exceptions to the rule, this philosophy just doesn't wash.

Understanding the Basics

It is the building of the business that requires a definite, albeit different kind of creativity. The sourcing of raw material or the components necessary to build the product or create the service is just another beginning. The equipment and the facility that will house and nurture the business are hardly secondary elements. The marketing concepts that will identify and deliver the customer base are still only at the beginning. Quality control and the method of distribution become mandatory aspects of business maintenance. And then, of course, there is the entire question of the dollars necessary to accomplish all those purposes. These expenditures often precede, by many months, the income that ensues from

> A good management team with a bad product is better than a good product with a bad management team.

these investments. Very much like advertising, the dollars resulting from a good advertising campaign don't normally get into the business's bank account until long after the expenditure has been made. Looking after the financial paperwork and making decisions that will protect the cash reservoir of the business are essential to the survival and success of any business. Those are just some of the things that the entrepreneur needs to consider. "The idea, by itself, is only the bare beginning of the game."

Can You Do It by Yourself?

Although it is true that you don't have to be a lawyer, an accountant, or a marketing guru to properly operate a business, you cannot afford to be in business unless you have a minimal understanding of these professions. And the best understanding is to recognize when you need help. To begin your business venture, you should speak with your professionals to ensure that you have the proper financial foundation for keeping books and records that will be both meaningful and understandable to you. Very much like a business plan, it must be a document that can be used as a helpful tool by you, possibly serving other purposes as well. Your accountant should also educate you regarding your current and future relationship with your bank so that you'll know what kinds of questions to anticipate when you need their help.

You should have the advice of legal counsel to be sure that you understand the nature of your leases—equipment leases as well as the lease for your business premises. Most people spend an inordinate amount of time worrying about the initial details of a lease without putting in the necessary time to examine the alternatives available when the lease expires. A good lawyer will ensure that you examine both the short- and the long-term relationship in that context. Your lawyer should also clarify any questions you might have regarding your incorporation, as well as all obligations and prerogatives with respect to partners, investors, and lenders.

Speak to your professionals early on to ensure that you understand the basic elements of law, accounting, and marketing before you embark on your business.

It's also a good idea to have the advice of someone knowledgeable about marketing and advertising; without it you may not be successful in establishing your customer base. It's all well and good to have a great idea for a business, but the idea is only the beginning.

Building the Framework

Even the simplest aspects of a business become another portfolio of responsi-

> A good business plan is a great tool to help you keep your focus.

bilities. Who is going to answer the telephone? Who is going to monitor the e-mails? Who is going to attend to the fax machine? The front office, in all its details, is a job in itself. To be sure, "it's lonely at the top." Even such mundane activities as opening the mail have got to be someone's responsibility. And then, the more critical activities such as fulfilling orders, handling a customer at the counter, and responding to problems are high-priority items during the course of the average business day.

Protecting Your Intellectual Property

The problem of outsourcing is that you will often be obliged to share with your "outsourcing partner" some of the proprietary materials that you and your company have developed. On the one hand, it will be necessary to do this in order for your partner to be in a position to perform his or her part of the "bargain." On the other hand, it is also important to ensure that your partner doesn't take advantage of this knowledge by utilizing it contrary to the relationship that you've developed. Whenever such a challenge presents itself, you must be sure that you've developed the appropriate paperwork, from a legal standpoint, to protect the proprietary nature of the information.

The Legal Approach

"It should be clearly understood that 'the widget product,' which will allow our two companies to function together, is a proprietary product belonging exclusively to Company A and that its utilization is designated for the sole purpose of completing the client project designated. Company B hereby acknowledges that it was unaware of the concept prior to our two companies creating the strategic alliance that will allow us to finish the project to client's satisfaction. Company B further agrees that it will not utilize the concept or any portion of the concept for any purpose other than that purpose designated in this agreement."

Although nondisclosure agreements or confidentiality agreements will contain many more specifics in terms of definitions, conditions, and contingencies, the above paragraph will give you an idea as to the core elements between the parties. Be sure to see your professional to ensure that the necessary nuances are properly defined between you and any other person or organization with whom you expect to share your proprietary information, or intellectual property.

Worksheet Questions

1. Why do you need to understand the equipment used in your business?

2. What do you need to know to be the "coach" of your business team?

3. Why is cross-training a necessary part of your business process?

4. What are some of the ways you can protect your intellectual property?

5. Is it a good idea to look for people to complement your own capabilities?

6. Is it the basic idea, or is it the implementation of the idea that makes a good business?

7. Why should you spend time with your salespeople making sales calls?

Business, Family, and Partnership

Watching Out for Your Partner
Another Story to Prove the Point

Calvin Justice and Julius Linspot were two engineers who were very unhappy with the firm in which they worked. As they described it, "More time was spent on silly, internal, political problems than on achieving the highest quality of our work product." Eventually, they decided to leave the firm and open up their own business. Although they didn't have a sufficient customer base to take big salaries, they were happy about the fact that they could spend all their time developing both their artistic and their business approach to clients. After a relatively short time, an interesting thing happened. Their business started to grow faster than they had anticipated.

What Was Next on the Agenda?

It became quite clear that they needed to develop a plan for the future of their business. The two partners needed to take a look at the future and decide how each of their goals and expectations could be fulfilled. Calvin had just gotten married and admitted to the expectation of one day having a family. Julius was married with two children and already facing the problems of "time with family," as well as the question of saving for education. The most imminent problem was that both partners were working many hours beyond the normal workweek and this had to be addressed immediately for the sake of family harmony. One suggestion was to cut down on the workload by not accepting new clients. This alternative could work in the short term but would be disastrous in the long term. Another suggestion was that they examine the possibility of making one of their employees a partner in the business. This would, at least, spread the upper strata of their workload to a third person. It was certainly a possibility. The decisive aspect of their conference was that family played a big part in their thinking, and that quality of life they sought would not be fulfilled if they kept driving down the same road. Both realized that, in the long term, being in a bigger firm would likely allow them to distribute their time in the best interests of their families. The question was, how could they handle this change and build value to a point where a merger or an acquisition might be realistic—without destroying the integrity of the business in the short term?

The Consequences of the Decision

With better than a year to go on their current lease, a discussion with their lessor was in order about a larger facility, expansion of their current space, or the prospect of leaving that space for a different area. With a year or so to go, there was time to discuss partnership with the third person, think about the money necessary for additional equipment as well as the larger facility, and examine the prospect of a new hire to handle the new clients knocking at their door. They recognized, as noted above, that these additional expenses would lower the value of their business in the short term but would definitely increase the value of their business, and their potential for being acquired by a bigger firm, in the long term. The partners agreed to move in this direction.

The Classic Partnership Picture

The above story represents the positive side of the partnership picture. There are many stories like this in which each partner is concerned about the other's welfare. Unfortunately, there are many other partnership situations where each partner is more concerned about his or her own welfare than the continuity and success of the partnership venture. Often the location of the business or the office becomes a point of contention because one partner lives farther away than the other. If this sounds like a silly argument to the reader, then you are on the right track. Any such problem can become bigger than it ought to be, if not resolved, and put the partnership in jeopardy.

> Partnering up can be a perfect solution to adjusting your business responsibilities.

Running a business by yourself is exhausting and leaves little room for letting up. The responsibility is constant. Having someone on whom you can rely to pick up the slack and give you breathing room is almost essential. An employee might, but he or she is not usually of exactly the same mind as the owner. Ownership not only has its privileges but often creates a greater initiative than mere employment. Throwing the ball without someone being available to catch it makes the game of business very difficult. You can't be on both sides of the field at the same time.

What's on Tomorrow's Agenda?

Most entrepreneurs are constantly facing both short- and long-term goals. The problem is that the short-term goals demand immediate attention and, if there are enough of them, the long-term goals get left on the back burner. But make no mistake about it, time has a way of passing quickly. When it's time to address the long-term goals, it may already be too late. Having someone else to pick up part of this responsibility is the saving grace of most entrepreneurs. It's called a *partnership*.

> Finding a partner you can trust who has complementary talents to your own can make life much more pleasant.

Taking the Fork in the Road

> You should be careful to be sensitive to your partner's emotional and financial needs.

There are many directions that a business can take. Some will put you on a road to growth and others will direct you to a path of stability. The problem is that one direction may be the right path for you and another may be completely wrong for the future of you and your family. It is very difficult to separate business from personal expectations. In the early days of a business venture, the time allocation can be devastating, and little time is available for the family. As time goes on, the time requirement for the business might not be as bad, but the habit is already formed. The family, unfortunately, still takes a back seat. It is all too easy to allow this to continue. But it is not impossible to stop. The problem is that you've got to make some conscious decisions. Failure to do so in time may, in hindsight, be the worst decision you've ever made. The concept of partnership can help to alleviate the pressures that create this problem.

I'll Think about It Tomorrow

It's one thing to say, "I understand, and I know that I need to address myself to this problem soon." It's quite another to take the bull by the horns and do something about it today. It is amazing how many tomorrows so quickly turn into yesterdays. Yes, it's important to work hard so you've got the money for your children's education; it's more important however to understand the kind of education they need. You can only understand this by knowing your children. And you don't get to know them by osmosis. You've got to spend the time. And before you can spend the time, you've got to allocate the time. And what about your other personal relationships? They also don't grow without a lot of help. Don't wait until it's too late. You've likely seen many situations where people waited just a little too long. Don't let yourself fall into that group.

> Make sure you don't let too many tomorrows turn into yesterdays. If you know you need to get something done today, do it!

The Alternative of Partnering Up

Partnering up can be an option for someone who is looking for a viable alternative to selling his or her business. It can also be a smart move for a buyer who doesn't want or isn't prepared to take on the total responsibility of operating a business with what he or she recognizes is something less than adequate education or experience.

The Synergy of Partnering Up

Many buyers recognize their dearth of knowledge in a particular field, or the fact that they have never been responsible for the totality of operating a business. They would like to contribute their expertise, whether technical, sales, or finance, but also need the comfort of knowing that there will be help available in areas that are unfamiliar. Think about the negatives to both buyer and seller and you will begin to recognize that an interesting alternative might be to sell part of your business to a partner, who can augment your experience.

Getting to Know You

"Diamonds are forever"—and partnerships are not! This is no reason to be frightened by the prospect; it is, however, good reason to exercise the appropriate cautions. You should always get involved in a diligent search to find out as much as you can about your prospective partner. You should always have a document between you that explains how you can separate, should it become necessary, without destroying the business itself. And you must always create a trial period during which you can determine if the synergy is right for both of you. Personality problems don't become visible until the two of you face some awkward decisions on which you might not agree. Developing a method for resolving these problems may be the key to moving forward on a day-to-day basis. In some cases, you will find that each of you should be in charge of particular areas of the company business based on the background that each of you brings to the table.

The Payoff Is On Results

If partnering up means that you have to give up a little income for the peace of mind you dream about; if partnering up means that you can work a shorter day or a shorter week and start to enjoy the quality of life you want so much; if partnering up means that you will only have to shoulder part of the responsibility of operating the business, then you may be on the right track. And in some cases, it is an opportunity to grow the business, which by yourself might be much more difficult.

Worksheet Questions

1. In what way is ownership different from mere employment?

2. When is a partnership more effective in terms of the long-term goals of a business?

3. Why is the time allocation in a partnership so important to the partners' families?

4. Why is partnering up a good alternative to selling in many cases?

5. How can the creation of a partnership avoid the need to sell a business?

6. Do you think it's a good idea to partner up if you find someone who has talents that complement your own?

7. Do you think that business partners need to understand each other's personal, family relationships?

8. Do you think it's better for partners to keep their business life separate from their personal lives?

9. When you reach a fork in the road in your business, are you always satisfied that you and your partner can agree on making the right decision?

10. How often do you think that you and your partner should reexamine your long-term goals?

CHAPTER 5

Bringing a Partner into a New Venture

Which Comes First:
Friendship or Business?

Jeff Schwartz and Byron Brown had been friends for years. They had often spoken of going into business together. When Jeff bought his first franchise, he made the offer of partnership to Byron who, at that time, had become an executive in a large company. Although Byron considered the opportunity, he felt that Jeff's first venture as an entrepreneur would be best served alone. After a while, Jeff increased his ownership as a franchisee and decided to create a new franchise group in another state. It was at this point that Byron decided to take the plunge. It was an interesting time because, even though Jeff had some misgivings about the franchise and its corporate activities, he had been successful in his first two ventures. Since the new state, California, was a successful venue for many franchise opportunities, both Jeff and Byron felt that this was a good time to create their partnership in this new area. Jeff would keep his existing franchises as an individual and the new franchises would be in the name of the partnership.

The Capital Involved

Both partners were aware of their different ownership percentages in terms of their individual investments. Jeff, on the one hand, had a positive cash flow from the two franchises that he owned individually. Byron, on the other hand, had accumulated some available cash. They agreed to put the same dollar amount into this new adventure in California. They had discussed all the differentials and agreed that this new venture was properly formed as an equal partnership. Along with the dollars involved, it was also agreed that Jeff had an existing knowledge of the business and an association with the executives at the franchise headquarters. This meant that much of Byron's time would be involved in catching up. This was also agreed to as an acceptable situation in the new partnership. Part of the reason was that Jeff would still be spending some time supervising his individual franchise holdings. Although it was anticipated that this might be of concern somewhere down the road, both partners agreed that it should not stand in the way of their new partnership arrangement. The deal was done. Both partners moved to California and proceeded to acquire leases for their two new franchises. And then, the problems began.

The Franchisor's Prerogative

The original business model established for the franchise appeared to generate a sufficient profit for both the franchisor as well as the franchisee. After opening a sufficient number of franchised stores to maintain continuity of the franchise concept, the franchisor started having problems in delivering sufficient inventory at the original wholesale cost. In fact, there seemed to be a problem in delivering sufficient inventory at any cost. The wholesale price of the merchandise started to rise . . . to the point where the original business model was no longer viable. Misgivings among the franchisees started to become verbal, leading to angry correspondence with the franchisor. None of this helped the situation. The franchisees wanted to source their own merchandise but the franchise contract precluded this without specific permission of the franchisor. In addition, the franchisees were reminded that, under the terms of the franchise agreement, the franchisor had the right to enjoy a profit as it transferred goods from the manufacturers to the franchisee group. With the increase in price for inventory (which the franchisor stated was beyond its control), the profit margin of the franchisor for being the middleman became a serious concern for the franchisees. As a result of the cost problem, Jeff's previously successful stores in other states started to make less profit.

The Inevitable Result

The new partnership was forced to recognize that, with the new business model and the high cost of rental space in California, the business was no longer viable. This was already being proven in the first store opened by the partnership. And unfortunately, the partners had already signed a lease in another shopping center although they had not yet opened the store. It was decided by both partners that this would be a good time to reevaluate their futures. They decided to pull out before their entire investment was gone. The problem was that they had already signed two expensive leases. The two leases represented an ongoing, long-term obligation of about $450,000, which was not eliminated just because they decided to close one store and not open the other. After many negotiations, the leases were finally terminated at a substantial cost. Jeff and Byron had their investments essentially wiped out. And even though the stores were no longer operational, they continued to face ongoing losses relative to the leases.

The Partnership

The most interesting part of the Jeff/Byron story follows. Although Jeff's original stores had also been negatively affected, they were still in business, primarily because their early leases had been less expensive than their California counterparts. The franchisor corporation agreed to help in the negotiations for the California lease terminations BUT only if Jeff agreed to "throw into the package" the two other stores that he owned outside of California. If Jeff did not agree to this, his partner Byron would bear one-half the brunt of the California debacle without the benefit of any offsetting profit from Jeff's other two stores. They were, after all, not part of the original partnership agreement. Jeff decided it was time to fold his cards and minimize the loss to the new partnership even at the expense of giving up his other stores as part of the settlement package.

> ### The Bottom Line Is Not Always Measured in Dollars
> It is certainly true that the decision was based, in part, on Jeff's loss of confidence in the franchisor/franchisee relationship. But his relationship with Byron was certainly a contributing factor. The partnership was dissolved; both partners lost considerable sums but the friendship survived. You won't find this happening very often, but when it does, it speaks well of the friendship.

What Percentage of Total Assets Is Each Putting In?

Although "being able to afford the investment" is a somewhat difficult analysis to make, there are certain parameters that need to be examined. Taking an

> Make sure you know the extent of your potential partner's financial capabilities.

additional mortgage on the family home might not be problematic. The question is: Were these dollars allocated to any other family expenditures? Was this money designed to be the basic fund for the children's education? Was the money to be available to a family elder who is not able to handle a health problem? You might say that these matters have nothing to do with you, and that you have no business getting involved in such personal aspects of your partner's life and lifestyle. And your partner may actually be offended at such personal inquiries when discussing the partnership. You may be sure, however, that your queries are both appropriate and necessary . . . even if the questions are not answered. This is actually a good-faith approach to the partnership, and will always remind your partner that you cared enough to ask.

Making Sure They Can Afford It

Enticing a person into a business relationship requires more than just an analysis of their business acumen or special education or specific talents. It requires an understanding of their motivations as well as their ability to handle the possible loss of their investment. You might think this is not your problem. But it is. A careful analysis of these matters, followed by a discussion with your family members, is advisable. You must be sure that your potential business partner has given the same dignity to the questions involved. If you don't, and the unfortunate happens, you may forever bear the brunt of his or her family problem. Although it is true that the business relationship ought to be clearly defined and be apart from the personal relationship, the reality of life suggests otherwise. The family, sitting in the bleachers, will invariably be involved in decision making, and cheering for the all-important profits involved. After all, a partnership is a business of two or more people working to make a profit.

If you know a person who shares your dream of success in a particular business, this might be the person you need at the other end of your playing field. If a problem arises, it is usually the result of a difference between your idea of success and theirs. You must guard against being blinded by friendship. The mutuality of camaraderie outside the business context might be much different when the time comes for making a business decision. You've got to be objective in your assessment of this person's talent, expertise, education, emotional proclivities, and discipline before making a decision. And even then, your assessment is likely to be skewed by personal aspects. If you know this person is a great salesperson and you are not, you could easily let this taint your judgment. But talent is not the only element that needs to be considered.

> Make sure you know at least the current goals of your partner and his or her family.

The Comparative Analysis

Understanding all the aspects of your own personality is difficult enough. Understanding someone else's is another story. You must understand that the context of your relationship with a family member or friend is entirely different from dealing with that same person as a business partner. The primary goal in the personal relationship is to establish an equilibrium, to maintain a continuity even in the face of adversity or conflict. The primary goal in a business relationship is to foster the concepts of growth and stability. The personal relationship in business becomes a secondary, albeit significant factor. It's a little bit like raising a child. Whatever the differences between the parents, the ultimate decision ought to be what's best for the child. Whatever the differences between partners, the ultimate decision ought to be what's best for the business.

What Is the Equivalent Experience and Expertise?

Some people may be more sales oriented than others but may not be in the category of a good salesperson. Others may be very mechanically oriented but may not have the experience or expertise that a particular business requires in that area. If one partner is actually an expert in one area of the business and the other is still a novice in his or her area, you will have a gap at the beginning of the relationship that may be difficult to bridge. There must be mutual

> Make sure you agree as to how business disputes will be handled.

respect, each partner for the other. Certainly, one partner may have been in accounting for many years while the other may have been behind a desk notwithstanding his or her special ability in sales, but this dichotomy must be understood and accepted by both partners. The biggest question will always be: What are the work habits and the emotional makeup of my

partner? If you can't handle this question, you'd better go back to the beginning. One person working while the other is staying home, is just not the best setup for a partnership.

Settling Disputes

As between any two people, it should never be expected that every decision will have unanimity. It is important that all partners understand this axiom. It is in this context that questions need to be answered within expeditious time frames. Business is built on moving forward, and any problem that stops or inhibits this movement is inimical to the best interests of any business. There is, of course, the philosophy that if you leave the problem alone, it will eventually go away. Any businessperson who operates this way is courting disaster. The truth is that most problems, left alone, will usually turn into much bigger problems. The best way to approach a problem is early on, while it is still within reach of an easy answer. The practice of mediation and/or arbitration may also solve these problems. They are so significant as to be handled in a separate chapter in this book. Be sure to read Chapter 19 before leaving this very significant subject of partnerships.

> Make sure you and your potential partner agree that the continuity of the business is your highest priority relative to business disputes.

Disparity Between Partners' Aspirations in the Later Stages of Growth

How do you resolve a situation where one partner wants to be a $1 million company and the other wants to be a $10 million company? What about one partner waiting to build the business for his children to take over and the other wanting to create a company that could float an IPO? How many other disparate goals are there, potentially? What about the business that is facing imminent disaster? How will the partners handle this? What are the exit strategies? It's impossible to examine these alternatives up front because people's needs and expectations, their dreams and their emergencies, will bring changes that could never be anticipated in the early stages of partnership.

Worksheet Questions

1. How can friendship be a hindrance to a partnership?

2. What does objectivity have to do with your assessment of a friend or relative?

3. How important are emotional stability and discipline to your partnership relationship?

4. What is the ultimate decision to be made in a partnership?

5. Why is an understanding of your partner's motivations an important assessment to make?

6. What is the definition of a partnership?

7. Why do you need to know the financial capability of your potential partner?

8. How do you expect to resolve business disputes with your partner?

9. Have you considered the alternatives in the event that these differences cannot be resolved?

10. Have you examined the different exit strategies that might be available in such a case?

CHAPTER 6

Bringing a Partner into an Existing Business

From Tentative Partner to Permanent Partner

Francine Simonetti had created, developed, and established a business of nutrition sports bars with a special formula for athletes. She had been in business for two years and had bootstrapped the business up to this time. (Bootstrapped means that she used her profit to reinvest in the business without getting someone else's money involved.) She had achieved success on a local level, but realized that in order to achieve that next level of success she would need additional help. This help could be at least one more person or the money necessary for a new hire. At one point, some investors wanted to buy into the company but, as often happens, the checks never got written.

They wanted to own a majority of the business by virtue of their investment, but Francine's business consultant suggested otherwise.

The New Partner

Ben Burnett had been monitoring the business since he was in college and, being a business major, he recognized its potential. Ben was very interested in joining the business but lacked the investment dollars required. He made an interesting presentation to Francine. He suggested that he work for the business for a year at no pay. On the basis of this good faith "time investment," he would be entitled to a percentage of the business. He was willing to sign a noncompete, nondisclosure agreement and to give up his stock on a prorated basis for failure to remain with the business over a certain period of time. In other words, he would start with 49 percent of the business, which he would keep if he stayed with the business for five years. For every year less than five years, he would give up 20 percent of the stock. And both parties agreed that if additional investors were needed, Francine and Ben would agree to a "dilution." Note the explanation below regarding dilution. In addition, there was the usual buyout prerogative of the remaining partner for any stock already earned by the exiting partner.

A Little Different Formula

"Incremental acquisition" of stock usually involves acquiring some percentage of stock for each year invested. This was the opposite approach, by getting the stock first (upfront) subject to giving it up in the event of a default in designated obligations. Essentially, it accomplished the same thing. But be careful here! One of the reasons that Ben preferred this approach was because of its tax implications. By getting his stock later on, when the business was worth more money, he would have a different tax liability. Here again, be sure that you get professional advice on this kind of transaction. There are many winding turns along this road, and having the best advice is important.

In the Final Analysis

It's a year later, and Ben is now a 49 percent partner with Francine. It is very clear that the arrangement has worked to perfection. They are moving to a larger facility. They have acquired additional equipment and their complement of personnel has increased. As Ben says: "Every day isn't perfect, and we have disputes that need ironing out, but our relationship has been strong and with enough trust to weather even the bigger arguments. We are doing very well. We are very busy. And no one could tear me away from this opportunity."

Do you think either partner needs additional protection? Do you think this kind of arrangement could turn into a disaster instead of a success? Do you think a lot depends on the ethics of the individuals?

If you've already embarked on your business venture, taking in a partner is less likely to be problematic in some ways. You have probably recognized where the holes are in your management fabric, and you are looking for someone with proven expertise to fill the gaps. This, however, does not eliminate the need for an objective assessment. There are many other important human aspects that form the whole individual upon whom will rest certain responsibilities for the success of the business. You can't afford to be casual about this human aspect when making this decision. There are a myriad of perspectives that must be examined, and you need to get a sense of "the whole person" before you make your final commitment. One approach would be to have a probationary period. This might allow you to make some of those important assessments before committing to a permanent partnership arrangement.

> Make sure you get professional advice regarding legal and tax implications when dealing with stock transfers in your business.

The Learning Curve

When starting a business together, as discussed in the previous chapter, an assessment needs to be made relative to the expertise of each partner and the role that each will play. When bringing a partner into an existing business, the roles are different. One partner has already initiated most of the protocols of the business. The new partner, however expert he or she may be in a particular field, will need to learn about the existing protocols in order to fit in to the scheme of things. The idea will be for the new partner to go through the learning curve and come up to speed in the quickest time possible. It's very much the same for an employee in a new job. Management is anxious for the new person to become effective on behalf of the business while also learning the job and how to relate to other members of the business team.

The Equity Positions

There are a number of reasons why the equity (ownership) positions of partners may not be equal in a venture that both partners start together. There are even more reasons when one partner comes to the party later than the other. Even if the "later" partner contributes a dollar amount equal to the shares of the business that he or she will own, the real sense of ownership will not kick in until both partners accept full responsibility for the success or failure of the business. This will invariably take some time. Defining the roles of each partner is difficult enough; understanding and accepting the responsibilities of each role is a real challenge. And the roles will change as time and circumstance dictate new challenges and responsibilities in the business. It is this process of adapting that will determine each partner's real role of responsibility. Don't expect this to happen overnight, but be careful to ensure that it does happen within an appropriate time frame.

Liking the Business

One of the questions you will face is whether your new partner will enjoy the business. Since you started the business and took it to a place where success was either achieved or was on the horizon, your involvement in the business will be unquestioned. Not knowing whether your new partner joined the business because of its existing or pending success will leave many questions unanswered. If he or she has never been an entrepreneur, taking responsibility for decisions of all kinds could be problematic. After all, you know the "good, the bad, and the ugly" of the business, so to speak. Your partner has yet to get a full dose of the realities involved in operating a business. It is for this reason, basically, that a consummated agreement can be problematic if you haven't given your partner some time to absorb and understand the nuances of the business. The other side of this coin is that if you don't get some kind of a guarantee or risk investment from this partner, your agreement will be little more than tentative. It is a challenge that each person must face when contemplating a partnership arrangement.

What If Your Partner Doesn't Like the Business?

In Chapter 21, we will examine the question of what might happen in the event that one partner chooses to leave the business, and how that partner's equity can be handled. In this case, where the partner's permanence is somewhat conjectural, and where the new partner will start off with equity in the business, it is appropriate to examine this issue in another way. Even though the partner may have invested the necessary dollars to "buy" his or her position in the company, you wouldn't want that person to leave the business and still hold on to that ownership position. Part of the reason is that you wanted someone to share the responsibilities of operating the business because you felt inadequate to handle everything by yourself. If you bring in the partner to help you operate, and end up losing the partner, you've not only failed to accomplish this purpose but you might be stuck with an absent partner who is still holding a percentage of the business. This might prevent you from being able to bring in a replacement partner. You might not have any more stock to sell. You can't let this happen!

The Necessary Buy-Back Provisions

A partner who buys into a business to become an active partner usually feels that he or she is certainly going to retain ownership of some portion of the company when they leave even though no longer participating in or contributing to the business. This is especially true if he or she has been there long enough to have participated in the operation and growth of the company. On the other hand, the exiting partner should understand that although he or she may be entitled to retain some equity based on the original agreement between the

Be sure to create an exit strategy for all partners that will not harm the integrity of the business when they leave.

partners, the remaining owner needs to have alternatives to maintain continuity and control of the company, and cannot have a mere passive investor in control of decision making. It is in this vague area that some alternatives must be examined. Note the differences between an "active partner" and a "passive partner," which will be discussed in Chapter 15.

Buying Back a Portion of the Exiting Partner's Equity

One way that this problem can be handled is to make arrangements to buy back the exiting partner's stock interest in the company. This ownership interest can be bought back in one of two ways: 1) By paying the dollars originally invested. This amount should not exceed the original investment until the business has achieved a certain minimum plateau in terms of profit or stability; and 2) If the partner has stayed long enough to have been instrumental in the success of the company and it has passed a minimum time frame (say, three years), then he or she would be entitled to have the business valued by a professional and have his or her portion of the equity paid out. The only concern is that the payout doesn't negatively affect the stability or continuity of the business itself.

> Make sure you understand how you can value "buy-back percentages," depending on the age of the business.

Diluting the Stock of Both Partners to Bring in Another Investor

Whether there is an exiting partner or not, there is always the concern that additional investors might be required to move the business forward. Keeping in mind that you can only share in 100 percent of the equity in a company, each partner must be prepared to part with some of his or her investment for the benefit of the business.

The alternative is to issue more stock (assuming there is authorized stock, not yet issued) to additional participants. This will result in the dilution of all equity holders when it is issued. As an example, if you increase the issued stock by 100 percent, from 1,000 to 2,000 shares, then someone holding 500 shares (which originally represented 50 percent ownership) would now have only 25 percent ownership. Anyone wanting to maintain control of the company needs to analyze this carefully. It's one of the considerations best shared with your professional early on. The alternative is to have the new investor buy stock from one of the existing shareholders. This, of course, creates other problems unless the existing shareholders agree to sell an equal percentage of what each owns. If the existing shareholders cannot agree to do this or if their initial agreement does not provide for this,

> How will a discussion of "dilution" help to reduce the problem when a partner leaves the business?

the control of the company could change. Whatever the arrangement is to which all partners agree, this must be carefully spelled out in the initial agreement. Trying to accomplish this expeditiously at a later time is usually a formula for disaster.

The Question of a Probationary Period

As with so many business problems, each alternative needs to be examined for short-term as well as long-term implications. In some businesses, a probationary period is appropriate for both parties before a commitment is made. On the one hand, allowing a prospective partner to learn all about your business can be risky. Allowing someone to learn all about a franchise, for example, may give him or her enough information to become a competitor instead of becoming the desired franchise partner. The same may be said of any business in which the owner gives someone exposure to all its nuances. One way to handle this is to have the prospective partner sign a noncompete agreement before starting on the job. In some states, this might not be enforceable but it will at least act as a warning and might prevent someone from doing something foolish. On the other hand, a period of probation gives the new partner an opportunity to find out whether he or she is really interested in the business and whether it's possible to work with the original partner on an emotional as well as an intellectual level. The same advantages obviously apply to the originating partner.

In some instances, the prospective partner might be willing to work at no pay for a certain period. This sounds like a good idea but, without the proper agreements in writing, it will not preclude the possibility of the partner

> Make sure your exit strategy always includes a noncompete, nondisclosure agreement.

becoming a competitor after learning the business. A great deal will depend on the nature of the relationship and the type of business involved. This caution should be a big one when considering the problem. One way to reduce the risk to some extent is to have the prospective partner put some money into an escrow account of some sort and hold the money until both parties make final decisions. The money may then be allocated to a stock purchase if the party becomes a partner, or the money may be released when it's determined that the party will not become a competitor.

The Question of Taxes and the Law

In any transfer of stock in a company, whether it is for anticipated services, for money paid, or for assets transferred, there are two challenges that need to be addressed. The first is that the transfer of securities (stock in a company) will often violate state or federal law if not handled properly by disclosures that may be required. Some of these laws are not so easily defined, and professional advice is always necessary. The other problem is that the transfer of any interest in a business venture may be subject to taxes. Getting advice from a professional in advance of any such transfer is another necessity. Trying to handle these questions without the appropriate background usually ends up as a mistake. Remember that the money spent on such professional advice will, more often than not, be insignificant compared to what conceivably could be a very costly problem if not handled properly.

The Majority Vote

In any new business venture that two people start together, the question of controlling the vote can be hard to handle. In an existing business, conventional wisdom suggests that, except in extraordinary circumstances, the original entrepreneur should have the controlling vote. This is usually based on the fact that he or she has already developed relationships with vendors, customers, and employees. The original person will likely have the best approach to resolving most problems within the company based on his or her knowledge of payment schedules, the ability to manipulate cash flow to the benefit of the business, and an understanding of the capabilities of people working for the company. Occasionally, there will be circumstances that mandate otherwise, but this is a good starting point. Also, keep in mind that the designation of an officer of the company may very well be a deciding factor, notwithstanding the 50–50 split in equity positions. Examine this carefully with your professional when putting the original agreement together. And don't forget to include mediation or arbitration clauses for the more pressing problems in operating a business. (This will be dealt with in Chapter 19.)

Worksheet Questions

1. How long will the learning curve be before a new partner can be effective in your business?

2. What is the problem with an equity partner leaving the business?

3. What are the alternatives if your new partner doesn't like the business?

4. How can you protect against a partner deciding to start a competitive business?

5. What are your partner's rights to retain stock if he or she leaves the business?

6. What kind of repayment for stock is appropriate in the first three years of the business?

7. What kind of repayment for stock is appropriate after the first three years of the business?

8. What is the primary concern relative to repayment for stock when a partner leaves?

9. Why should discussion of "dilution" be considered in the early days of a partnership?

10. Why should a securities professional be consulted in any stock-transfer situation?

11. Why should a tax consultant be consulted in any stock-transfer situation?

12. How does incremental acquisition of stock usually work?

13. What is the caveat about allowing someone to learn all about your business?

Putting the Partnership Together

What Can You Expect from Your New Partners?
Two Stories to Prove the Point

Mark and his brother-in-law, Abel, decided to form a partnership in a mobile-oil change business. It was agreed that because the business was new and would take some time to get off the ground, Abel would keep his job and Mark would devote his full time to this project. They had heard that many small businesses had started this way. In fact, spouses often start a business this way to ensure that their family income will be stable in the early days of building the business. Abel would contribute time and energy as required, providing it didn't interfere with his primary job. After six months, it became apparent to Mark that this was a labor-intensive business, that the earnings were based on an hourly charge, and that with one vehicle, this would always be a one-person business. Abel might not make a lot of money, but he wouldn't be doing any work to earn it, either. Mark might pay some profit to Abel but it would always be from money earned by his own hard work.

Does this partnership make any sense? Should Mark have done a more careful study of the business before embarking on this adventure? What was Abel's contribution to the business? When Mark decided to terminate the business, Abel was very angry. Abel felt that after a while, the business would be able to purchase a second vehicle, at which time he would join the working partnership. Mark's attitude was that the business would always be labor-intensive, and that it would be difficult to build equity even over the long term. Which person do you think had the right idea? Do you think they discussed this before Mark started working? Do you think they should have?

Juan and Kip started a small publishing business in Mexico. They were selling children's books, created by local artists and poets, to grandparents who visited the country. They traveled together and were actually having a good time while increasing sales of their books to little shops all over the country. Since there was no countrywide distribution system in Mexico, this was the only way to build their customer base. The market was big enough for expansion but in order to achieve growth, Juan and Kip would have to travel separately in order to double their customer contact. Kip understood the need for separate traveling but Juan did not. Juan's idea of a partnership was spending time with his partner, even at the expense of making more money. Since there wasn't enough money to support Kip and his family, they had to close the business. Kip moved back to the States and the business venture was over.

- What did the two situations above have in common?
- Would the partners in either story have agreed to work together if they were aware at the outset of just what was involved in growing the business?
- Do you think these people did enough research before starting their respective businesses?
- Do you think this research would have made a difference in either case?
- Do you think that potential partners ought to understand the financial needs and expectations of each other before they venture into a partnership?

Forming a Partnership and Making It Work

Does Each Partner Have the Same Goals?

As an entrepreneur, you must understand that each person has different short-and long-term goals. Some people are actually looking for a good job with sustained longevity, regardless of the pot at the end of the rainbow. Some people are interested in building a dynasty and don't want to be deterred by short-term or interim business activities. Still others are interested in exiting the business with a multiple of their investments in as short a time as possible. Try to get a sense of what your partner has as his or her long-term goals to avoid having your expectations fall by the wayside for failure to factor in your partner's position.

Setting Yourself Up to Fail or Succeed

Many times the secret to a successful business venture is not in the concept; it's in the details. This is why a business plan, in advance of the business's operation, is essential. Frankly, one reason to create a business plan is to decide whether or not the business concept is even viable. Conceptually, it is easy to envision the success of an idea. On a practical level, however, it is impossible to properly appreciate the elements on which the success of a business is predicated without putting them on paper and doing an objective analysis from every aspect of the business. It is a good idea to remember that old axiom, "The devil is in the details." Don't ever take this concept lightly. It is the very essence of survival and success in the business world.

> All partners must have an understanding of each other's goals and expectations.

The Fear of Failure

What makes the entrepreneur tick has always been a question with a strange dichotomy in its answer. It seems that most people function on the basis of either greed or fear. More often than not, the fear element is predominant. It is the fear of failure that forces the entrepreneur to expend his or her best energies to accelerate or maintain the growth of the business. This involves the fear of failing in the face of people watching you—a disaster to the ego. It involves the fear of not being able to support your family; the long-term prospects are disheartening. Worst of all, it evokes the fear of losing whatever capital you've used of your own or from others, suggesting the possibility that you may never have the opportunity to test yourself again. You should never underestimate the power of the fear involved in forcing more and more work, more and more time involvement, out of the available hours in a single day. It's very much the same as the athlete who calls on new strength and energy when it appears that she is really at the end of her rope. It is, in fact, the reason why some succeed while others fall by the wayside. It's also known as winning or losing. Don't deny the validity of this fear syndrome in your own business life. Is your partner motivated by fear or greed? Does it make a difference?

Although the "fear of failure" will not likely be eliminated, given that it is in the very nature of the individual, it is clear that proper preplanning will lessen the negative emotional impact of the fear syndrome. You will at least have developed a plan. And having a plan is like turning the light on. All is revealed . . . at least at the outset. And much of the fear is gone. You should share this with your partner at every stage. Both of you need to fully recognize all the elements on which the success of the business will likely be predicated.

The Partnership Relationship: Putting It All Together

Every business venture, usually at some point in its initial growth cycle, requires the talents or investment of more than just the single creator who first generated the momentum. The relationship of these two or more people is often the predicate for establishing the division of labor, the prerogatives and obligations of each party, and the essential synergy that results in the team effort. This relationship comes in all sizes and shapes.

The Usual Beginning

Many of the conversations start in a very casual fashion. The entrepreneur familiar with operations recognizes the need for a sales-oriented partner, or a group of partners recognize the need for additional working capital . . . and the conversation begins. At the outset, the goals and basic elements of the relationship appear to be simple. "You do this and I'll do that." Who should have the final say in determining the direction of the company or, for that matter, even its day-to-day activities? What happens if one partner wants to exit the company? Will the return of a partner's investment leave the company in jeopardy with regard to its necessary working capital? What about the hiring of other people and the allocation of responsibilities? What happens if one partner is a workaholic and the other partner wants more personal time? Should there be a difference in salaries? The problems can even devolve to some simple basics that hardly appear important at the outset but can fester until they become difficult, if not impossible, hurdles to overcome. What happens when one party decides to buy a van for both personal and business purposes while the other partner decides to drive a Jaguar? The devil, indeed, is in the details.

Synergy vs. Authority

The purpose of partnership is to ensure that the things one partner can't handle will be handled by the other. This doesn't mean that this division of labor requires a hands-off attitude by the partner not specifically responsible for a particular piece of business. It does, however, require that someone be in charge without the other constantly intruding in the decision-making process. Sales, for example, might involve hiring people, deciding on a marketing plan, and designating advertising dollars. It is clear that these decisions affect all other parts of the business and require at least a tacit approval of the other partners involved. Conference, analysis, and agreement will always be significant parts of the partnership mix.

> Conference, analysis, and agreement are the keys to a successful partnership.

The Biggest Word with a Capital T

When people get together in a business context who have not worked together before, there is no way that they can anticipate the extent of the other's involvement. In many cases, in fact, each partner will not necessarily know the extent of his or her own abilities until they have been tested in the context of a continuing business environment. It is this experiment in experience that enables people to grow into their responsibilities, accept the many diverse challenges of the day-to-day business activity, and—ideally—exceed even their own expectations. The fact is that in practically every business, the job requirements will constantly change.

The Peter Principle

In some cases, the level of expertise required may very well exceed the abilities of the person who was perfectly capable of handling the job in its early stages. This is the time when adjustments are made to ensure that expectations can be realized. The biggest asset that each person can bring to the business is total and complete trust worthiness. It is *trust* that is the real bottom line to every relationship. When you don't have to look over your shoulder or be involved in the micromanagement of every aspect of the business, you have achieved the first level of success in any company. If you find this in a partner or an employee, you have come to the gates of success with a team that has every reason to move from one successful plateau to the next.

Hiring a New Person

Every business is constantly changing and, one hopes, growing. In this context, you will be constantly reevaluating your business concept, your personnel, your financial capability, and your expansion potential, to name but a few of the daily intellectual activities of the average entrepreneur. The hiring of personnel is one of the most delicate aspects of this changing landscape. The bringing in of a partner is even more delicate.

The Trust Doctrine

The most significant thing of all is the ability to put responsibility on partners' shoulders that they can handle without needing to be supervised at every step. This is part of the trust factor that is the core element in the hiring of any prospective employee or in forming any partnership. If you have an opportunity to inquire about the person, ask if he or she is candid, proactive, and willing to assume responsibility. If you feel comfortable asking, a good question that covers a multitude of virtues and sins might be: Can this person be trusted? It is an open-door question and will give the respondent an opportunity to think carefully before answering.

The Fear Aspect of Business . . . and How to Handle It

Most businesses don't start as giants. They start with an idea generated by an individual. The idea germinates and becomes the core of the business concept. Along with this germination, the entrepreneur usually recognizes that a variety of tools are needed. These will include personnel, money, and talent. In some cases, the business has an excellent start with the obvious potential for future growth. In other cases, the idea just seems to jump into gear, based on a little bit of luck and some surprise momentum. The interesting thing is that neither kind of business is necessarily on its way in or out of the woods. If you're examining this with a potential partner, be candid. Anything less than full candor can be interpreted as a sales pitch and will forever be a problem between the partners.

What Are You Looking For?

One of the funniest statements you will ever hear is, "I'm glad to be leaving the corporate world and going to work for myself: less pressure, more time for my family, less aggravation." For those of you who have already embarked on the ship, USS *Entrepreneur*, you will likely be laughing. If you're just starting to think about it, take this caution from the old musical standard: "It Ain't Necessarily So." If this is the quality of life you dreamed of, don't let anyone stand in your way. But make sure your partner's ambitions are consistent with yours.

> You must understand that you are giving up a certain comfort zone when you leave the corporate world to enter the entrepreneurial marketplace.

The Confidence Factor

In your past corporate life, you probably had a job you had pretty much mastered. You probably worked within a certain

> You must understand that partnerships are based on compromise and the ability to adjust expectations.

set of parameters and had confidence in your ability to shoulder the known responsibilities. As an entrepreneur, all bets are off. You might be dealing initially with a business about which you know less than you'd like. You'll certainly be involved with a myriad of details, none of which you had ever been asked to handle in your old job. There will be marketing, selling, margins, financials, production, customer satisfaction, advertising, and on and on it goes. If you can't handle it, you'll need to get someone who can. This costs money and will dilute whatever profit you depended on to take care of your family. Make sure your partnership involvements will alleviate the problems and be sure you're willing to share the profit to achieve this.

Enjoying the Game

Success, of course, comes in many different packages. Some packages are filled with dollars and an equal amount of aggravation to go along with them. Is this the idea of success you dream about? Then there's the package that contains less money and less aggravation as well. There's also the package that allows you to enjoy your family and your leisure time, but may give you less income than you enjoyed in your former corporate life. Acknowledge that it is unlikely you will find a package that contains it all. Life is composed of equations . . .

> Remember that a partnership is usually a long-term involvement.

compromises. On balance, you need to give something up in order to enjoy something else. Make sure you know what will be your best game plan for maximum enjoyment before you start on your new adventure. It's always best to check for water in the pool before you go off the diving board. And your partner's goals, although not the same as yours, must at least be complementary.

Worksheet Questions

1. Why is it necessary for you to realize that each person has different short- and long-term goals?

2. Why is it necessary for you to factor in your partner's expectations when contemplating the development of a partnership arrangement?

3. Is greed or fear a motivating factor in your personality, or your partner's?

4. In what ways might either of these motivations be problematic?

5. Are you aware that the division of labor, together with the prerogatives and obligations of management, will be the keys to a successful team effort?

6. Do you feel that trust is a high-priority quality in a successful partnership?

7. What happens in a partnership if the partners need different levels of compensation or responsibility?

8. Do you think you can handle any disputes within the partnership without the problem jeopardizing the business?

Keeping Your "Real" Partners in the Game

When You Lose Sight of the Important Things

Alan Barfeld had lived in the Northern California area most of his life and was very familiar with the Silicon Valley industrial complex. As an inventor, he had achieved myriad successes with a variety of sophisticated devices. Since the computer industry was another exciting place to make money, he took on the job of developing a "soft glass," which would be superior to the elements prevalent in the industry at that time. He was successful in creating just the kind that would dramatically improve product reliability. After developing the prototype, proving the concept, and filing the appropriate papers for patent protection, he decided to start his company.

Putting the Pieces Together

Alan considered himself an entrepreneur and felt that he and his team of two sons were perfectly capable of developing a company to accommodate all the elements of sourcing materials, manufacturing, marketing, and distribution. He was bright enough to recognize that, not having developed this specific type of company before, seeking professional advice would probably be a good idea. He made arrangements to examine his entire concept with a professional to ensure that he and his sons were on the right track. What the consultant found was a plethora of potential problems.

Although his son Leonard was an experienced salesman, his knowledge of the complex computer industry was very shallow. In addition, due to the lack of capital and the absence of cash flow, Leonard had to leave Minnesota and move in with his dad for the duration. Leonard's family became unwilling partners in the venture without their prior consent.

Alan's other son, Jeff, was very mechanical and Alan felt that he could run the manufacturing end of the business. Unfortunately, Jeff's expertise did not extend to setting up and managing a manufacturing facility. He had no experience in sourcing materials or pricing components. In addition, due to the income constraints, Jeff also moved in with his dad, much to the chagrin of his wife and five children, who were left in North Dakota. Jeff's wife and children also became unwilling partners in this business.

The Professional's Advice

The consultant's advice was predicated on the above items plus many years of experiencing the struggles and the outcomes of a variety of businesses. She suggested that, since the soft glass was protected by a properly filed patent, getting into the marketplace in the shortest time would be the best course of action. This meant approaching a manufacturer with the capability and the distribution system already in place. This would move the concept into the marketplace expeditiously, and Alan and his family would be able to license the rights to the manufacturer for a percentage of product sales. Although Alan appreciated the rationale behind the advice, he chose to take a contrary course. He decided to maintain control over all the elements of the product: the manufacturing, the selling, and the distribution. Unfortunately, by the time he had positioned himself to start the company, the proverbial bottom fell out of the industry and his business had to file bankruptcy.

The Lesson to Be Learned

Although it is only human for the entrepreneur to think positively, these three, father and sons, had not examined the other side of the coin. All were excited about the prospect of working together. A more conservative approach, however, would have meant more to all three families. Alan had to sell his house and move to a less expensive California suburb he could afford.

Jeff had to return home to a pending divorce—and his wife's statement: "If you're going to be away to *play business*, you certainly haven't got time to "play house."

Leonard's financial situation had become critical. He had used up the children's education savings and was on the brink of bankruptcy.

Did all this need to happen? Would a more careful and objective analysis of each person's abilities have made a difference? Do you think that greed played a part in this scenario?

The family still gets together at Christmas. Do you think their get-togethers have been affected by this family business history?

Family Members as "Partners"

The dream of some entrepreneurs is to someday be working side by side with a son or daughter. Indeed, the dream of some sons and daughters is to someday be working with a father, mother, aunt, uncle, or other member of the family from whom they can get a jump-start in understanding how to properly operate a business. The idea is to ensure that this dream does not turn into a nightmare as it did with Alan, Jeff, and Leonard.

> Make sure that each family member understands and is willing to participate, despite possible limitations in income and quality time for the family.

The Problem with Expectations

"Know thyself" is a difficult enough imperative for everyone. Knowing someone else, however close the relationship may be, is certainly a horse of a different color. What you see in the family or social context is not necessarily a preview of what traits you may encounter in a business environment. And when the reality falls short of your expectations, the problem becomes obvious. There are parents who recognize that their son or daughter is entirely too aggressive and opinionated to be successful in a corporate environment where discipline and conformity are the prerequisites for moving along. These traits, on the other hand, might be perfect for an entrepreneur whose creative abilities are more important than his or her willingness to conform. Obviously, care must be taken to ensure that these traits are integrated in a way that makes them effective.

Working with Family

Be careful about pulling family members into your business scenario. If you need their help, be sure that the parameters are carefully constructed. Be sure that he or she is a willing and eager participant, not an indentured servant. And be sure to give them the authority that's commensurate with their ultimate responsibilities.

Set Standards

A good start is to set standards with your significant other, your children, or your spouse or partner. Make it clear what your position is about allocation of time for both business and personal matters. But even more important, make sure you have an understanding of their expectations, and that you feel comfortable about being able to maintain consistency in that context. Take a look at your calendar. Check for planned holidays and the needs of family members with whom you've promised to spend those days. Don't go into a business venture without seriously considering the consequences of these dynamics. Once you're in, you may not be able to make the appropriate changes without diminishing either the business or your family. And remember that a partnership is one of the significant ways to split the time, the obligations, and the profit. Be aware of how each affects your life, both positively and negatively.

> Don't forget the difference between "quality of time" and "plenty of time."

One of the most fundamental aspects in starting a new business is to ensure that the family can keep food on the table while dollars are going out and might not be coming back in as quickly. Examining this with a spouse, significant other, and children is an essential element that is often pushed aside at the beginning and can quickly become the center of controversy. Make sure that each family participant is willing to be a player, fully aware that profits may take some time to generate and that time can no longer be devoted strictly to quality of life. A business has time frames and emergency allocations of its own. You and your family must be prepared to understand this dramatic dynamic.

A Question of Priorities

Everything becomes a question of priorities. Conflict may arise when an important family situation collides with a serious business operation and both require your full and immediate attention. Which is more "immediate," your daughter's confirmation or your computers being down? Your son's track meet or your best customer in town? Clearly conflicts such as these are significant. But look at the minor ones, too, the ones that, by themselves, are not disastrous. Coming home late for dinner . . . constantly. Or not coming home at all. No available time with the children. It forces you to ask that age-old question: What is this really all about? Do you think that Jeff's family and Leonard's family were asking themselves this question?

It's the Old Equation

It is certainly a balancing act. You can't do without the wherewithal to support the family, but what's the point in supporting the family if you're not involved in its growth and stability in an emotional sense? Owning your own business is a prerogative for some, an obligation for others. But even in the latter case, you still have to make some choices. Hiring a key employee to give you some quality time with your family will undoubtedly draw some dollars from your own income. You might not be able to buy that place in Vail, Colorado, but you will have the time to take your family there. Which, indeed, is the more important of the two? And what about sharing both profit and responsibility with a partner? To what extent do you think this would help or hurt your situation?

Quality Time vs. Plenty of Time

The question of quality time is relevant whether you work for yourself or for someone else. It is a question of allocation, not availability. If you concentrate on the necessity of time for the family, you will probably do so regardless of the time requirements of operating a business. If you have not already determined this time allocation in your personal life, you will not likely develop it automatically as an entrepreneur. Be especially careful about this! Get ready to recognize the difference between a stop-everything emergency and a problem that can be handled by an alternative method. The imagined emergency at your business might turn out to be a real emergency at home.

Worksheet Questions

1. Why should you make sure that each family member participates in the decision to go into business?

2. Do all members recognize the reality of "business time" versus "family time"?

3. Are they all willing to make the appropriate adjustments relative to time with family?

4. Have you examined the priorities of family and business?

5. Do you honestly feel that you can properly allocate your time to both family and business commitments?

6. Do you know the difference between quality time and plenty of time?

7. If you bring a partner into the business, do you think that you should be careful that you both hold similar goals and expectations—especially if he or she is a member of the family?

CHAPTER 9

Getting, Using, and Protecting the Money

The Incremental Investor

Anthony Blair started a business venture: a contract manufacturing business. His concept was attractive to investors, and a number of investors agreed to jump aboard. As time went on, the usual scenario unfolded. One investor had a couple of previous investments "go south" and couldn't afford to move forward with the plan. Another potential investor claimed to have family problems and couldn't take the time to follow up. A third investor got advice from her broker that a more stable portfolio would better suit her. And the last investor, as often is the case, decided to go forward with the project but with a little more caution than the original investment program called for.

Bill Lewiston had made his commitment based primarily on his personal experience with Anthony. Unfortunately, his legal counsel suggested a somewhat more cautious investment in the enterprise. Bill agreed to hedge his bet. He agreed to put some of the investment upfront and the balance in subsequent increments as the business grew.

In many cases, this incremental investment approach is based on a business reaching a certain plateau of success within designated time frames. In this case, partially because of the personal relationship (and partially as the result of Bill's legal advice), the increments of investment were left in limbo without any defined parameters.

Instead of the total investment being held in escrow (a holding account), subject to certain levels of achievement, it was left to Bill's discretion. Anthony wasn't terribly concerned because he knew that Bill's dollar reservoir was deep and that Bill was not subject to acting on a whim.

Unfortunately, the business hit a couple of bumps and the cash flow was negatively impacted for a short time. This caused Bill to feel uncomfortable about completing his promised investment in the business. Interestingly, the cash-flow problem was corrected but only after Bill had decided to curtail further investment. Anthony was left in a bind.

- Do you think that an escrow with a defined sequence of investments would have made Anthony more secure?
- Do you think that an incremental investment program is a good idea for an entrepreneur?

The Incremental Investment

Many investors are interested in investing in your business in a way that will best protect their investment. One of these ways is to offer a certain dollar amount upfront with the understanding that if you reach a certain plateau of success (that is, if you achieve certain things within the time designated in your business plan), they will follow their initial investment with a second investment. There may even be a sequence of incremental investments that they will make, based on your achievements. With a program of this nature, you are, in many ways, subject to the discretion of the investors. It might not be a good idea unless the investment dollars are held in an escrow, which releases automatic payments on the achievement of certain business successes. Be sure to examine this with your professional, and be certain that you can meet the prerequisite achievement.

The usual reason for a partnership is to fill an empty space. In some cases, this empty space is filled with money; in others, it is filled with the expertise that the original owner lacks. The alternative to sharing your equity position as an owner is to borrow the money and hire the experts. In some cases, it is clearly better to borrow the money and buy the expertise than to share the long-term success of your dream. Making this determination often depends on the time frame involved. Sometimes you can wait; in other cases, you must fill the empty space or become vulnerable to failure.

Sharing the Equity vs. Borrowing the Money

Accessing the money necessary to kick-start a business is a time-critical element. Without the dollars, one can find it difficult, if not impossible, to proceed at all. The question of borrowing or accepting the investment dollar becomes the first decision to be made. When you borrow from a bank, the lender will usually take a security interest in all of your assets in the event that you fail to make the payments on the repayment schedule. This means that the bank, or other lender, has the right to seize all of your assets to satisfy the obligation if you fail to pay. Taking all your assets, which might include hard assets such as equipment, or other assets such as intellectual property, patents, licenses, and the like, could prevent your company from functioning at all. This is something to consider.

On the Other Hand

The alternative to borrowing is to allow someone to invest in your business, to own a part of the equity of your business, to be your passive partner by being entitled to a portion of the

> Make sure you know the difference between borrowing and accepting an investment in your company.

profit that the business generates. These investors will not normally hold a security position in any of your assets. On the other hand, unlike a bank or lender, which will monitor your progress just to ensure that you are capable of repaying the dollars borrowed, the investor will be much more interested in the incremental growth of the business. They will want to be closer to the decision making than a lender would be. They will, in fact, be looking over your shoulder, not just in the short term, but forever. Keeping in mind that investors can also be very helpful, it is certainly a consideration that needs to be examined from all perspectives.

Inviting a Partner or Hiring an Expert

It should be clear to the reader, whether you are an experienced entrepreneur or not, that no one person is capable of performing all the myriad tasks necessary to properly operate a business. It is imperative, therefore, that you understand the contents of your own "toolbox" and recognize those areas in which you are weak or inexperienced. When you can do this, you will be in a position to know what kind of person or people you need to round out your business team. The next question is: How can you meet these needs? Essentially, you have three choices. You can hire the appropriate people as employees. You can retain outside companies to fulfill those needs. Or you can bring a partner into the business. You should examine these alternatives carefully, because one aspect of your business might suggest one of those alternatives, and another aspect might suggest another.

Hiring the Person

If you know that a person with specific expertise will need to be on board for the long term, and that you can afford the necessary salary and amenities, then hiring will likely be your best choice. This person will bring that needed expertise to the business team without intruding on the variety of other decisions that you want to keep exclusively in your domain. In time, you will be able to decide whether this person has the ability and the inclination to expand his or her talents to other aspects of the business. This gives management an opportunity to build the various levels of the business team so necessary to the success and continuity of any company.

Retaining the Outsource

There will be other times when the need for particular expertise is important in the short term. By outsourcing the problem, you will pay only for that time, those hours, that the business needs. You will not be worrying about amenities, such as health insurance, vacations, and the like. You will be able to take complete control over just which portions of the responsibility you want done and the time frame involved. In addition, you will be dealing with people who are already experts in that particular field. This will eliminate the time usually involved in training. A good example is a fulfillment house that is responsible for the warehousing and distribution of product. It also eliminates the need for additional space to hold and protect your product. The offset of dollars may be more beneficial than you might think.

> Make sure you know the differences between hiring personnel, utilizing an outsource, and bringing a partner into your business.

Bringing in the Partner

There are many reasons to discard both the employee and the outsourcing method of enhancing your business team. One reason may be that you need someone to share the full responsibility of ownership. This means that your partner will have put something at risk dollars or other assets. With something at risk, most individuals will tend to take the decision making more seriously. They will be looking not only at the short-term problem but at the long-term implications as well.

The Differences between the Alternatives

You should be prepared to analyze the many dimensions of your potential partner before signing on to a partnership agreement. In some cases, they may seem like partners and when all is said and done, they'll do their job (provided they get ten minutes for coffee every hour and an hour for lunch) and they'll work as long as they're there. But they won't take on the same responsibility

> Make sure an exit strategy is included in your original partnership agreement.

that you will . . . as you have to. There's another problem: you don't know these things at the outset. Even a probationary period might not do it. They'll work their tails off for the 90 days—but after that, watch out! "I'm going skiing." Is there any magic? No! But caution should be on the table.

On the other hand, if you hire someone, it's a quid pro quo until that person is no longer needed: you will pay and they will function for the designated period of time. If you partner, you will have a permanency to your relationship even if you end up terminating the employment of your partner—which you, as the CEO or president of the company, would be entitled to do. Make sure there's an exit strategy in place so that you don't end up with an unemployed, equity-holding hanger-on. There are a variety of ways to create these situations and the question will be handled in great detail in Chapter 21, "Diamonds Are Forever; Partnerships Are Not."

Protecting the Partnership for the Long Term

The process of two people starting a business together, even when a perfect synergy appears to be the case, requires some consideration of potential problems. After all, in the long term, it is the continuity of the business that is, or ought to be, the highest priority.

In the following case, two people decided to get advice from a business consultant. Once the preliminaries were properly examined and, presumably, agreed to by both parties, the consultant put together a memorandum to counsel, which would allow an attorney to follow up the agreement with the appropriate formal paperwork. This would result in the bylaws of the corporation or the operating agreement in an LLC. The memorandum that follows suggests both the questions and the answers of the parties involved. It is typical of the kinds of problems that need to be anticipated in any partnership arrangement.

Memorandum to Counsel

"The purpose of this memorandum is to facilitate the preparation of a partnership agreement between the two parties, Bob Halder and Amy Onderstein, to operate a company called Solemn Dreams. A meeting was held on August 26th for the purpose of examining a variety of issues that needed to be resolved by and between the principals (hereinafter referred to either as 'the parties' or 'the principals') in order to establish the guidelines of an agreement. Although not all elements were discussed, the following should represent the basic predicate for a partnership established within the appropriate protected legal environment: LLC, subchapter S corporation, or otherwise."

Predicate for the Partnership

"The parties have been working together at this venture for the past one-and-a-half years and have decided that each has made an equal and substantial contribution to the effort in terms of both time and dollars. As a result of the above, acknowledged by both parties, it is agreed that compensation to each principal shall be equal, on the assumption that both will be devoting full time to the building and maintenance of the company. This shall be by salary, benefits of any and all kind, as well as distribution of profit."

Equality of Decision Making

"Without going into the specifics of price equivalency and investment, suffice it to say that there was an extensive discussion of stock participation and, although the concept of different classes of stock was alluded to as well as an examination of a cap on expenditures (both mentioned later in this memo), it was agreed that neither should have the singular, ultimate decision-making prerogative on any subject. An examination of each party's involvement reveals that, at this stage of development and based on the mutuality of thinking relative to the future of the business, neither should be solely responsible for making decisions that will affect the company in the long term without the consent of the other party."

The Tie Break Resolution

"As a result, it was agreed that ownership of the company (equity participation) shall be 50–50 and that designation of a president or other officer of the

Make sure you make arrangements for a method of resolving disputes in your original partnership agreement.

corporation (whatever the final legal entity) shall not change the decision-making prerogative being shared equally. The ultimate 'tie break' will be represented by an arbitration clause, choice of one arbitrator by agreement, or each to pick one and the two to pick a third, if necessary. It was clear that such a tie break would be used only in those instances where the two can't agree on either a decision or a third-party advisor. Legal language for this section is left to the judgment of counsel."

Failure to Actively Participate

"Although it was agreed that each would hold 50 percent of the equity of the business, the question of active participation in the business needed to be resolved. It is anticipated that each would devote essentially full time to the business. If one of the principals decides to exit from the business or spend substantially less time in the business's operation, leaving the other party to hire or retain personnel or to seek an outsource capability to handle the business normally handled by the absent party, any such expense shall be deducted from the compensation owed to the absent party. Should this deduction be insufficient to cover the costs of replacement personnel or outsource, the money put forward by the remaining party shall be considered a loan to the company. This loan will have a priority position and will be repaid before any additional compensation (salary or profit) is designated to the absent party."

No Third-Party Sale for Three Years

"In the first three (3) years of the business (from the date of incorporation), neither party will have the prerogative of selling his or her shares to any third party; any buyout, one of the other, shall be strictly on a negotiated basis. Subsequent to the third year, each shall have the right of first refusal should the other party decide to sell."

Retention of Majority Interest by Remaining Partner

"However, the selling party MUST sell 1 percent on a pro-rata basis, relative to the price being offered, to the other party. That is, the selling party cannot transfer more than 49 percent to any third party or group representing a third party. The purpose clearly is to ensure that the remaining party retains a controlling interest, and the clause relative to equal decision-making prerogative shall be eliminated at the time of transfer."

> Remember that the most important element for an entrepreneur is to maintain control over the decision making in his or her company.

Valuation of the Business

"The valuation of the business at this time shall be by a valuation expert to be agreed upon by the parties or, in lieu of such agreement, by each appointing an expert, the two experts then appointing a third. Two of the three experts must then agree on a valuation of the business at that time, or the two closest will be averaged to establish the value of the business. Consideration must also be given to the business's ability to make the appropriate payments without jeopardizing the integrity of the business itself and its ability to maintain its continuity in the face of these payments."

Assignment of Intellectual Property

"All intellectual property including, but not limited to, the web site and any software created for the purpose of maintaining the company's financial or selling records, the logo, and any other appropriate or necessary 'mark,' shall be transferred to the company by both parties. A further understanding must be noted that any additional intellectual property created during the partnership shall be the property of the company."

Assignment to the Business

"All business assets currently owned by either party and held for the benefit of the business shall be transferred to the company's new legal entity. Whether the legal entity shall be an LLC, a subchapter S corporation, or any other shall be determined by the parties in conjunction with advice of counsel and the appropriate financial advisor. This is a serious question considering that each of the parties may have special needs that require separate consideration."

Some Basic Precepts

"At least some of the basic partnership protections should prevail in the agreement although they were not discussed at any length during this meeting. They would include the normal protection of two signatures being required for any withdrawal or expenditure exceeding a certain amount, and two signatures required for any contract or extension of contract exceeding value of a certain amount."

Possible Investors

"There was also a brief discussion about a third-party investor holding the 'vote' (with one of the parties) should both give up a portion of their equity position to allow a third party to enter the venture. This was not discussed at length other than to indicate that a different class of stock might be the answer. In some way, language ought to be inserted that would avoid this problem. This question, and its implications, could also have an effect on the particular legal entity established for the business, and should be discussed with legal counsel."

Key Man Insurance

"In the event of the death of either party, the question of 'key man' insurance has been discussed to prevent the remaining party from inheriting a new partner."

❑ ❑ ❑

As you can see, the creation of a partnership requires a great deal of thought with respect to a variety of short- and long-term goals, expectations, and resolutions. Although it is impossible to anticipate all problems, the best approach is to attempt to analyze at least those questions that exist at the time of the partnership's foundation.

Worksheet Questions

1. How can an entrepreneur generate money for the business?

2. Is it better to borrow from a bank, or to sell an equity position in a company?

3. What vulnerability do you face if you borrow from a lender?

4. What is management's vulnerability to an investor?

5. What is a "sequence of incremental investments"?

6. Why is incremental investing a potential problem for management?

7. Why is it important that a partner have dollars or other assets at risk?

8. What can you do if one of the partners exits the business, or chooses to spend less time on it than you?

9. How does a remaining partner protect against the sale of a partner's interest to a third party?

10. What is an exit strategy and why is it important to have one in the original partnership agreement?

11. What kind of insurance does a partnership need to avoid inheriting a partner when an original partner dies?

Trust

Difficult to Earn, Easy to Lose

Misrepresentation:
Inadvertent or Otherwise

When Barney decided to sell his business, his intention was to maintain the highest level of candor and honesty. This was, in part, based on the fact that the purchase price would likely be paid over a period of time and anything less than an honest presentation could be detrimental if the buyer felt that any deception was involved. Barney had created a unique packaging device that allowed many small businesspeople, especially those who were selling over the internet, to package and ship their product with ease, with little time and labor, and with minimal cost.

Although the device was susceptible to breakage with severe use, the concept was viable and Barney built a substantial business in only two years. He offered the business for sale through a business consultant. His feeling was that a broker would be interested in the commission whereas a consultant would be interested in long-term protection because the purchase price was to be paid over a three-year period. The consultant stressed the need for total candor in order to achieve a situation where the purchase price would be fully paid.

The parties met at Barney's house and one of the questions asked was how many devices were returned due to damage. Barney's answer was "less than 1 percent." The question was asked again at a later time and the answer remained the same. The business was sold.

After six months, the buyer called to say that his experience with returns was 10 percent, not the 1 percent that Barney had represented. Barney's answer was that he meant 1 percent after the original returns were repaired and sent back to the buyers. This explanation did not wash with the buyers because the cost of repair-and-return, although not extensive, had not been factored or calculated into the price of the business. A lawsuit was threatened for misrepresentation. The matter was ultimately settled. Barney had to forego 25 percent of the purchase price because of the deception.

❑ ❑ ❑

- Do you think Barney thought this was merely an oversight, an inadvertent error, a misunderstanding, or do you think it was an intentional deception to increase the purchase price?
- Do you think the revelation of this additional "minimal" cost to the new owners would have changed the purchase price during negotiations? Do you think it would have been 25 percent of the purchase price?
- Do you think this should have been disclosed during negotiations?

The Slippery Slope

Trust is built over a period of time. Consistency is the key. Consistency leads to dependability—the knowledge that the answer will always be true. When even the slightest trace of doubt enters the equation, dependability is out—

consistency is out and trust is no longer the standard. Building trust is a long, tedious journey. Rebuilding trust is a much more difficult road to travel, a much bigger mountain to climb. When you achieve that pinnacle, don't lose it by making a silly mistake like Barney.

Trust Is the Highest Priority

Whether you hire, or borrow, or decide to share equity, there must be mutual trust on both sides of the fence. It's not so much the money that is important. It's the confidence you need to have in a person to whom you've given the responsibility for decision-making participation. That person, in turn, whether a lender, a partner, or an employee, must have sufficient trust in your ability to keep the pace you've set. They can neither outrun you nor fail to keep up with you. There must be a mutuality of understanding with regard to the most appropriate direction for the company at all times. In every business, at every level, the question of trust should be "top of mind." It is not something that happens by accident and it certainly doesn't happen overnight; it is an intellectual commodity that has to be earned.

> Trust is the highest priority in the spectrum of business activity.

Straight from the Shoulder

There are a variety of elements that constitute the basis of trust. One of them is candor. The thing that most management people are looking for is a person who can be honest about how an outcome was achieved, whether the result was positive or negative. It is certainly not expected that every decision will have a positive outcome. People who don't make any decisions are not likely to make mistakes. These are not the people on whom a company usually depends for its success. People who are constantly making decisions have the law of averages against them; they will invariably make errors in judgment. These, however, are the very people on whom the success of a company usually depends. Remember, failure is not a way of life; it's a moment in time! Get over it, and use the experience and knowledge gained to your advantage when the next decision needs to be made.

The Key to Dependability

Trust is also based on dependability, and most dependability is the result of consistency. The people who can be depended upon for quality decision making are usually those on whom management relies for their best business directions. This doesn't mean that the person is always right. It does mean that the person is always accountable and is willing to accept the responsibility of accountability. It is interesting in most businesses that if you want to get something done, you should give it to the busiest people you have. They will usually find a way to get it done. They understand the nature of prioritizing; this is part of the consistency that puts them in the dependable category.

The Boy Who Cried "Wolf"

Many business situations may be viewed as serious to one degree or another. There are those who immediately push the panic button and scream for help. These people who cry "Wolf" when the matter can actually be handled simply and expeditiously are hard to take seriously because you never know if the sky is falling or not. Those who understand when help is really needed can be depended on to reach for help when it really matters. As you can plainly see, trust is earned on an incremental basis. It takes time, experience, and responsiveness. When you find an individual who can be trusted to work consistently in the best interests of the business, that person becomes accountable, extraordinary, and valuable.

Breaking Your Word

Building the foundation of trust involves a number of things. The person's word becomes "as good as done." When the word is broken, the entire trust process fails. It is as good as it gets when you find it, and as dangerous as it can be when you've lost it. Trust in business is not a secondary issue; it might be, in fact, one of the core issues in the building of any business. Look for it, nurture it, protect it, and be thankful that it comes along at least once in a while.

Worksheet Questions

1. Why is trust something that must be earned over a period of time?

2. How does trust, which is earned, convert to additional responsibility?

3. Why is occasional error not critical to a person who has earned the trust of management?

4. What are some of the elements that constitute the basis of trust?

5. How is dependability the result of consistency?

6. Why is trust based on dependability?

7. Does dependability suggest that a person is always right?

8. Does dependability mean that the person is always accountable?

Review Cash Flow Constantly for Growth and Profit

Don't Forget What a Partnership Looks Like

Sam and Lily decided to pool their money and buy a piece of property for investment and maybe for income as well. They bought a condominium in a small mixed-use building. It was close to home and they thought it could be for fun and profit. When they executed all the paperwork, they didn't realize that they were getting involved in more than just being the owners of a condo. They thought that the monthly condo dues would take care of all the details of the common areas.

When they attended their first meeting of the condo association, they began to get a different picture. Although there were only five others in the building, the same situation prevailed as in much bigger associations. Some people wanted to spend more money than others on the garden. There was discussion of fixing the garage doors, painting the white lines in the outdoor parking area, and installing a stanchion to protect the side of the building from drivers who didn't pay enough attention when making the swing into the garage. Even though the building was only a year old, there was some paint that already looked a little old. And then there was the plumbing problem in Condo #3 that no one could find the answer to. Was this the responsibility of the owner of Condo #3, or was it a problem that affected all the owners and that all the owners would be responsible for? The last item on the agenda was that the manager, who was hired by the owners, felt that he wasn't getting paid enough salary. In other words, there were many decisions to be made. The question was whether the monthly condo dues would be enough or whether the owners would have to contribute additional money to handle some of these other aspects of property management. It was clear that the building not only had to be properly maintained, but also needed to be upgraded whenever possible. Although this was a high priority for most of the owners who lived there, Sam and Lily recognized that they had an interest in upkeep and upgrading as well. A better-looking building meant that they could ask a higher rental.

Although they didn't realize it at the outset, they soon recognized that the condominium association was a partnership in which they never expected to participate. Do you think Sam and Lily would have changed their minds about the purchase if they knew the degree of financial responsibility and management time they would need to devote? They realized that if the majority wanted a dollar assessment in addition to the monthly dues, they would be obliged to comply. What if an owner couldn't afford the additional investment? Do you think the additional money could result in a lien on their condo to be collected by the group when the condo was eventually sold? Do you think that this resolution would be included in the condominium association regulations? Are you interested in buying a condo after reading this story?

What Is Cash Flow All About?

Forecasting cash flow is especially important regardless of what your profit-and-loss (P&L) statement may look like at the end of the year. After all, the P&L statement is usually developed on the basis of sales made but not necessarily collected, and purchases made but not necessarily paid for—the accrual concept. On the other hand, cash flow represents the actual dollars spent vs. the actual dollars collected—the cash concept.

Although cash flow is particularly important in a seasonal business activity where there are many months without substantial sales, most businesses need to address the subject for other reasons. When buying product for resale, hiring a salesperson, or even creating an advertising campaign, it is essential that you anticipate the dollars needed for the expenditure long before you expect to earn the dollars to repay this advance expense.

Working on the basis of day-to-day requirements can be terribly problematic without the necessary cash availability. If you need to buy inventory or parts, or start making payments on equipment or additional personnel, these dollars will be spent in advance, sometimes significantly in advance, of the money ultimately generated by sales and profit. Without a working capital reservoir (money in the bank), you must have a lending source that will take you over this financial hurdle. This will invariably mean a relationship with a lending institution that allows you to borrow money in one fashion or another. A simple loan is one approach. A line of credit is another.

Creating a Cash-Flow Analysis

Every lender will want to understand the reasons for this temporary financial problem and they will insist on seeing a cash-flow forecast. The best forecast will obviously be based on the previous year's activities . . . providing, of course, that you've had a previous year's activity. If you have no such history, your forecast needs to be backed up by assumptions that are credible and believable based on the marketplace and with the support of purchase orders, existing inventory, and the like.

What you need to do is create the future of the business in financial terms. Any sophisticated businessperson (including a lender) is aware that a new business will not likely generate an immediate profit. The question is: When will it happen? By creating a future year, based on serious and credible investigation, you should be able to show how long it will take for the business to reach its break-even point (the point at which income is equivalent to the costs necessary to produce that income).

However successful a business may appear to be at any moment in time, the emergence of a surprise always holds the potential for disaster. The solid management team is always prepared. And the best preparation is to monitor the position of the business constantly. This means to develop a business plan that suggests what the financial position of the company should look like at various stages of development. The biggest consideration in this monitoring should be the cash position of the business. Anticipating the deposit of receivables is the first level of cash priority. Anticipating the need for additional equipment or personnel is a second priority. And the ability to accommodate any cash need comprises the third level. Don't be taken by surprise by failing to make the necessary and appropriate adjustments to both the short- and long-term positions of the company.

> Always review your cash position to ensure proper credit and collection protocols.

Receivable Turnover Period

Whatever the nature of the business, whatever the P&L statement may show at the end of the year, the key to the current status of any business is the cash flow. Buying the appropriate inventory or raw material or component parts to maintain continuity of a business is a delicate balance. Even the purchase of equipment comes into play as part of the cash-flow challenge constantly going on in any business. You must be careful, at all times, to ensure that the expense against revenues is adequate to maintain products and services, as well as anticipate the needs of the business on a day-to-day basis. On the other hand, you must also be sure that expenses against revenues don't deplete the cash ability to function. After all, customer success notwithstanding, you must be able to pay for goods, services, personnel, rent, and lease payments even though your receivables might be a long time turning into cash. Watching the cash flow of a business is a high priority. If you're going to be an absentee owner with the responsibility of the business's operation on the shoulders of someone else, you'd better monitor the company's activities in two important ways. You must be sure that the receivables are being given the appropriate priority. You must also ascertain that you're not falling behind in such mandatory matters as taxes, rents, and commodity purchases. Without maintaining a careful watch on these necessary expenses, you can't be sure whether the profit is "clean" or whether unpaid bills will negatively affect it. And if you're in a partnership, ALL partners must be aware of these basics. You cannot abrogate your responsibility by assigning it to your partner. It isn't fair. It isn't smart. It isn't good business.

The Nickels and the Dimes

Daily business activity has a way of demanding that you take care of the minute-to-minute problems. This leaves little time to examine the long-term effects of not paying adequate attention to how you can improve many of the items you're dealing with.

In better times, when your margins for profit were substantial, or at least adequate, the "little dollars" were allowed to fall through the cracks. In today's economy, you need to conserve dollars to maximize your profits in every way. The "little dollars" have become more important. Just as "the man" says: "A billion here, a billion there. After a while, it adds up to real money!"

> You should constantly monitor your costs against revenues to be sure that dollars are not falling through the cracks.

The Little Dollars

On the noncommercial side, you might think you're saving money when you purchase household items from the big wholesale houses. You can save on many items by buying in bulk. The problem is that, although you might be saving money on the individual units, you have dollars sitting on your shelves until you need the balance of the goods. It might better serve you in tight dollar days to buy just the goods you need at a higher price per item, and use the balance of the dollars for other purposes.

On the Commercial Side

In better times, you probably let your operating expenses grow because you were generating greater profits on your goods and services. This might be a

> Review and revise your business plan on a periodic basis.

good time to take a look at some of these expenses. Sales, administration, and marketing are some of the areas where there is silent and constant growth. After a while, if you fail to take appropriate precautions, some of these expenses will accelerate. For example, in general office activity, you get used to using the same office-supply vendors. After a while, you depend on them to acquire just about everything you need, never stopping to think that your own staff might save dollars by sourcing many of these goods themselves. The bigger items might involve renting or leasing equipment instead of using those all-important dollars to buy capital equipment. Less obvious savings might be found in comparing UPS, DHL, FedEx ground, and independent carriers to find the least expensive way to transport goods within the necessary time parameters. Doing a cost analysis should not take a lot of time, and your efforts might represent a serious savings. Remember, "A billion here, a billion there."

The Bigger Costs

As for insurance policies and employee benefits, it has probably been a while since you did any kind of cost analysis on items of this nature. With costs having increased dramatically over time, it should not surprise you that there are savings to be had. Perhaps the biggest potential for savings might be in the use of internal sourcing for personnel instead of just calling an agency and paying a commission. Another might be in outsourcing certain of your activities instead of insisting that all personnel activity be performed inhouse. Contract labor vs. recruitment costs can represent some big dollar savings.

Don't Close Your Eyes

In today's business marketplace, it pays to revert back to the nickels-and-dimes approach to see if the barn door can be closed before the horse is gone. Some of the bigger expenditures are for trade shows, advertising, PR, and the like. Although it might be shortsighted to curtail any or all of these outlays, it is certainly a good idea to revisit the question of what kind of advertising and marketing would be the most cost-effective in this particular economy. Don't be surprised if many of your workers have ideas about cost savings that might never have occurred to you or your partner. It's always good to ask the people on the front line.

Movin' Too Fast

In track, you learn that if you try to run faster than your legs will move, you will fall flat on your face. The advantage to being a hurdler is that you must take the same number of steps between all the hurdles. This pacing allows you to maximize your speed without going beyond your capabilities. In business, the same rules apply. Building too fast can force you to move faster than your reservoir of dollars and personnel will allow.

Learning to Go with the Grow

Business develops at different speeds depending on a variety of factors. Sometimes, growth is dynamic because a local competitor goes out of business or merely moves to a different locale. At other times, growth is generated because of cheaper access to raw materials across the globe. Most of the time, growth is based on the fact that a company has succeeded in establishing its brand in the marketplace and has built a customer base through image, service, and quality over a period of time.

As growth takes place, it will often bring changes to the entire structure of the company and, in many cases, in the levels of responsibility of the different individuals throughout. Their willingness to understand and accept these changes will tell you about the adaptability of your personnel—and their ability to function within a different envelope of authority. Make sure that you and your partner are on the same page in this regard. Even in day-to-day activity, the manager of a print shop will likely put a big print job on the photocopier instead of the press. It saves time. The owner would more likely put the same job on the press instead of the photocopier. The profit margin is much greater.

Changing the Protocols

Credit policies may be stricter as the company grows and needs its cash flow to be more consistent. Having the dollars available for the purchase of goods for resale or for the purchase of raw materials to build inventory is essential for the growth of the company. You can't sell the goods if you don't have them. On the other hand, you don't want inventory on the shelf that you can't sell. This is the typical predicament of almost every business. And always keep in mind that the longer you wait for your money, the longer someone is holding onto it—using *you* as their bank. The cheapest way to borrow money is to pay your vendors late. However, ask yourself if this is good business before you adopt it as a method of doing business. The long-term implications could spell trouble.

Spending in Order to Earn

In the early stages of the business, you will be spending money and probably not earning an amount equivalent to that expenditure. Each month, spending more than you're earning, you will go deeper into the hole, using the investment dollars. This will represent a cumulative loss. The lender expects this to be the case. What the lender wants is a credible projection of the time when you have not only reached the break-even point, but also earned back the dollars spent in the days of little or no income. This will give the lender (and you) a time line. If this time line is realistic, you will start developing a profit when that time has arrived. This is the beginning of your success at your new venture.

> Learn to anticipate the time frame necessary for expenditures such as advertising and selling to generate sales and profit.

Although this may represent a fairly simplistic view of the lender relationship, it should give you an idea as to just what to consider when contemplating borrowing. It is clearly essential for you to take advantage of professional advice to ensure that your presentation is consistent with the financial requirements of most lenders.

Counting the Nickels

In today's economy, it is imperative that you consider every expenditure on behalf of your business. The fact is, every savings is not necessarily in the best interest of the business. The strategy involved in cutting costs must be carefully examined in the face of the current economy, as well as with a look to the future.

Cutting into the Future

If your facility appears to have more space than necessary, making arrangements for a smaller area might be appropriate. But before you make this decision that might impact your ability to properly service your business in the future, consider the possibility of leasing some of the space to another business for a limited period of time. This might allow you to recapture that portion when it becomes necessary. In addition, there are many businesses that could be interested in having space available to them without having to sign a long-term commitment.

Cutting Again into the Future

Another cost-cutting approach is to eliminate personnel during the time business is at a low point due to the economy. You are not likely to cut key people, because your current business profile probably depends on them. Be careful, however, of two important business problems, even with people who are in secondary positions in your business. The first is getting the people back when business resumes. The other is the possibility of someone familiar with your business approaching a competitor with ideas about potentially acquiring some of your existing customer base. Neither of these situations is in the best interest of your business.

The Nickels for the Dollars

Very often, in the interest of cutting costs during a downturn in business, some executives with little or no real experience have a tendency to cut wherever a nickel appears to be unnecessary. In some cases, saving the nickels will lead to a rift between management and labor, causing unnecessary tension where none needs to exist. Cutting jobs at one level, thus causing other employees to be under additional pressures, is a bad precedent. The other aspect of maintaining profit is to be careful that it doesn't look like management just doesn't care. The fact that management has enjoyed a substantial profit during the good times is not a reason to maintain the same substantial profit at the expense of the people on whose shoulders rests the responsibility for maintaining the company's success. Management must always recognize the difference between survival and success. It must factor in the essential needs of the labor force. It should never appear that the health insurance for employees will suffer in order to maintain the yacht or the mountain resort facility for management.

Monitoring Your Margins

It is said that business may be likened to a child. Like a child, it requires constant attention and is subject to change at almost any time. Whatever the legitimacy of this idea, it is certainly clear that the only constant in business is change. One of these changes is the all-important question of whether the goods or services you offer together with your price points are still appropriate as you seek to retain your position in the competitive marketplace.

In the First Place

In the printing business, for example, printers used to offer wedding invitations in the early days of introducing "instant printing" to the new residential customer base. It was, in fact, a good beginning for those who knew nothing about the new technology that made this sort of expeditious printing available. It was rather complex, because it involved a variety of details that called for discussion with the customer to be resolved: the quality of the paper, the size of the type, the style of the type, the color of the ink, the size and particular fold of the card in question—to name only some of the items involved. It was an opportunity to meet the customer and get to know the person. It was a time involvement that could run as long as an hour or more. Many times, the parent and the prospective bride would need to confer, before, during, and after the discussion with the printer before a decision was made. And many times, specifics would be changed and, sometimes, changed again.

Cost-Effective Time Frames

The time involved in these consultations was rarely compensated appropriately by the profit realized on the sale. Yet even today, printers are constantly increasing their capabilities by offering more and more collateral products and services. They have equipment that creates prints so enormous as to completely cover walls and windows. They have equipment that can reproduce from digital cameras. They can take discs and e-mails from computers anywhere in the world and replicate them in full color for distribution. They have machines that duplicate computer discs and DVDs for marketing and advertising purposes. The question that each owner must ask is, which of these products and services are cost effective from the standpoint of the time involvement, as well as the cost of the equipment?

Even in the Manufacturing Sector

Even in the manufacturing sector, the question of time and money spent for each product demands that the owner decide if the products are producing a cost-effective, bottom-line profit. If your personnel are spending 50 percent of their time building a product that is producing only 10 percent of your profit, the question needs to be asked. This is true especially if the other 50 percent of their time is responsible for 90 percent of your profit. It may be time to do a painstaking reappraisal of your entire selling position in the marketplace. You may be sure that your competitors are revisiting questions of this nature every day.

The Components Are "Over the Top"

It is equally important to note the cost of component parts that represent the products or services being sold. Over time, costs have a way of creeping up due to any number of reasons without management being aware of the change. In some cases, the change seems insignificant enough until the differential hits the bottom line. By that time, it may be too late to make the appropriate adjustments. One of these components is delivery. At one time, you may have charged for delivery. To meet competitive demands, you may have converted this charge to a "courtesy." As you examine the cost and maintenance of a vehicle, together with a competent driver, insurance, and gas, you may see that your ultimate profit may have been eroding without your even realizing the difference . . . until the negative impact began to hurt.

Remember the Name of the Game

The name of the game is profit. If you are a smart businessperson, you will be looking at your P&L statement periodically to ensure that your costs against sales are being maintained at the level that allows you to enjoy your profit. When delivery charges or increases in rent or the costs of new vehicles or additional personnel or stronger advertising start to eat away at your profit picture, you want to be in a position to anticipate this in order to make the proper adjustments. The question of margins in the products or services you offer is in the same category. Make sure that you are paying as much attention to the one as you are to the other.

There Is Light at the End of the Tunnel

Many businesses suffer in some economies. If you were able to build your business in the first place, it is quite likely that you'll be able to build it again as time heals the wounds that caused the downturn. Remember that there are many ways to handle problems. Don't think that just because you can't understand all the alternatives, you need to shut the doors. There are people in the business community who have faced these devils before and survived. Seek out the advice that will help you get back in the game before you decide it's too little, too late. There is light at the end of the tunnel. Remember, "Failure is not a way of life. It is a moment in time. Get over it and move on!"

Worksheet Questions

1. Why is monitoring cash flow so important in operating a business?

2. What is the receivable turnover period?

3. Is it better to have inventory on the shelves, or cash in the bank?

4. Why should you be doing a cost analysis periodically on the administrative costs of your business?

5. Why is it sometimes better to lease equipment than to purchase it outright?

6. What is the difference between the accrual system of accounting and the cash system?

7. Why is it important to understand the difference?

8. Why should you be careful about cutting back in an attempt to save dollars during a bad stretch?

9. Why is it important to monitor the costs of component parts and raw materials on a periodic basis?

10. Why is it important to redo your business plan periodically?

11. To what extent must all partners pay attention to the cash flow of your company?

The Joint Venture or Strategic Alliance Is a Partnership

Is a Partnership Your Only Choice?

Alice Bekel was an architect who had raised a family and built a business practice in such a way as to realize success in both areas. She used a guesthouse on her property as her business venue and outsourced most of her detail work instead of buying the equipment necessary to handle it inhouse. This home-business approach enabled her to build a successful, profitable business because her expenses against revenues were kept to a minimum.

She had bid on a number of jobs together with Jack Morganthal, who was also a successful architect but who had built his business in the more conventional way. He had leased or purchased all the equipment necessary to handle every aspect of a job inhouse. He had rented office space and hired the personnel appropriate to a growing architectural firm. Alice and Jack had been working together in this way for about five years. Their basic reason to consider a more formal partnership relationship, to which both agreed, was that the presentations they made together were always more successful because they complemented each other's expertise. They thought that this would make a good foundation for a legal partnership. They met with a business consultant and discussed the matter at great length.

There was no question that the synergy between these two people was dynamic. They had proven it a number of times with successful bids. The problems that they faced as prospective partners were entirely apart from their business synergy. Since each had devoted different energies and made different investments in the building of their respective businesses, the question of business value became an issue. Alice had historically devoted less time to her business due to family commitments and expected to continue with this splitting of her time. Jack's intention was to devote "full time plus" to the new venture as he had been doing with his own business since its inception. These two issues caused much concern. Since the profit of both businesses was essentially the same, the value of both businesses was also essentially the same, notwithstanding the investment made by Jack. There was an adjustment of salaries and profit relative to time spent by each, but solving this unique problem was a matter that left a variety of other questions open and unresolved.

The partnership was formed. The partnership lasted six months. The partnership was dissolved. Although synergy is one of the most significant aspects of any legal partnership arrangement, it is not the only element on which a successful partnership is predicated. Fortunately, most partnerships in joint ventures or strategic alliances don't depend on such a personal relationship. It's more business than nonbusiness, and has a different set of principles on which to base its existence.

❑ ❑ ❑

- Which of the partners do you think was more disenchanted with the arrangement?
- Do you think the parties could have adjusted their expectations and made this partnership work?
- Might there have also been questions of control involved in this situation?

Synergy: 2 + 2 = 9

The question of filling a slot in the business that requires certain expertise has already been discussed. There is another side to this issue as well. When two people or two businesses work closely together, they can usually generate significantly more activity as a team than they could have working separately. This is called synergy, and it is the main reason why any two people or entities find greater success in working together to accomplish almost any purpose. In fact, in many cases, one person or entity might not be able to even bid on a job without the complementary talents of the other.

Whenever there is a "codependency" as described in previous chapters, all of the partnership philosophies prevail. These relationships usually depend on both entities doing the same thing at the same time, or one entity being responsible for getting something done on which the other entity will piggyback its subsequent activity. Without these things happening within the appropriate time frames, success may very well slip through the cracks for one or both organizations. While recognizing that neither holds a superior position to the other, it is imperative that both parties meet their obligations in a timely way.

> Be especially careful about the time lines of your joint venture partner that could preclude performance of your end of the agreement.

The Joint Venture or Strategic Alliance

There is nothing suggested in the words "joint venture" or "strategic alliance" other than what appears. There is no special paperwork that creates either of them nor are there dramatic protocols that make them work. They are merely relationships in which one party is able to piggyback on the other so that both parties have an advantage that neither, alone, could otherwise enjoy. If one company has the hardware to handle a particular job and the other company has the software essential to the job, neither could take on the job without the input of the other.

The Problem

Since neither company is knowledgeable enough about the other to know its inner workings or management style, these relationships are usually based on reputation. This does not mean that the people from one company working with the people from the other company are necessarily going to get along famously. This potential problem must be addressed in a variety of ways. The first is to ensure that each company knows just what responsibilities it is responsible for. Since the work of one company may be predicated on prior work for which the other company is accountable, the time frames for each project must be carefully spelled out, and failure to perform in a timely fashion must carry serious consequences. Although money damages will often provide this incentive, in some cases, failure on the part of one company could easily lead to failure of the entire project. If the foundation is never built, the walls will never go up. Part of this problem can also be addressed by insurance bonds, which could have some bearing on the ability to hire substitutes in the event that one company fails to perform as expected.

The Legal Approach

One way to avoid a lax attitude on the part of either of the joint venture or strategic alliance participants is to set very definite requirements within very specific time lines. Failure to complete their part appropriately will cause a default and a forfeiture of a dollar amount to accommodate for the failure. Contract elements of this sort are mandatory for such relationships.

Nondisclosure with Penalty: Liquidated Damages

In many cases, it is appropriate for each company to discuss its capabilities with the other. This may often require the disclosure of information about protocols, personnel, or proprietary information that the company ordinarily keeps secret. If this kind of information is disclosed, two things must be kept in mind. The first is that the information be kept to a minimum and clearly labeled as "private and confidential" or some other cautionary language. It should also be delivered in conjunction with a nondisclosure agreement worded to protect against disclosure of any kind. In many cases, the people to whom it is disclosed should also sign individual nondisclosure documents.

Legal Protection

Language similar to the following caveat should precede any such proprietary information disclosed.

Keystone Confidentiality and Nondisclosure Agreement

Private and Confidential Caveat

The information contained in this business portfolio is being disclosed for a very specific purpose. There has been only one original presentation prepared for management. This original should be kept in a private, safe, and secure venue to ensure that its contents will receive the dignity of being maintained as PRIVATE AND CONFIDENTIAL.

It shall be the responsibility of management to maintain this security in order to establish and ensure the confidential nature of its contents. If management decides to share the presentation with any person or persons other than the management team itself, they shall duplicate the presentation, give it a specific number, put it in a secure envelope, explain the confidential nature of the material in writing, have such confidentiality acknowledged by the appropriate signature of the responsible party, and otherwise protect it from being further distributed or disseminated in any way.

Such caution shall be exercised both inside and outside the corporate environment with the understanding that the material disclosed is for the benefit of the management of the company and for the singular purpose of preparing for a potential joint venture between the parties.

A confidentiality and nondisclosure agreement is usually prepared for protection of very specific proprietary information. You will note the caveat above, which is suggested to precede any disclosures in writing. Although violation of this kind of agreement is difficult to prove, it is an essential document between the parties. If nothing else, it inspires an intimidation

> Make sure to have all parties sign the nondisclosure, confidentiality agreement to protect the proprietary information disclosed to your joint venture partners.

Always have your professional, your attorney, examine any joint venture agreement and any nondisclosure, confidentiality agreements.

in all who read it. The following agreement is an example of the simplest of these agreements. As with most agreements, it can be as long or as short as you choose, and its size and content will usually be commensurate with the level of protection you hope to achieve. The agreement below is particularly short because, without more specific requirements, it is difficult to address items in detail. These may include specific copyrights, trademarks, patents, personnel resumes, job categories and responsibilities, and the like.

Confidentiality and Nondisclosure Agreement

This is an agreement, effective June 1, 2007, between ABC Corporation and Keystone Inc.

Background

Keystone is anxious to examine certain specific information for the purpose of deciding whether or not to enter into a joint venture agreement to create The Master Matrix for the Commonwealth of Massachusetts. Since ABC regards this information as confidential, ABC is willing to disclose this certain specific information, but only under certain terms and conditions. In consideration of the said disclosures, Keystone agrees as follows:

Terms

"Confidential information" generally means information that is regarded as confidential and may include but not necessarily be limited to the following: business procedures, customer identities, technical material, and concepts, plans, financial information, protocols, personnel, and procedures. Confidential information shall include information disclosed to Keystone within one year from the effective date of this Agreement in writing, and shall include that information which is disclosed orally to Keystone and which appears to be material in nature and goes to the essence of the business requiring protection. Confidential information shall be deemed to exclude information that

a) is in or becomes in the public domain without violation of this Agreement by Keystone; or

b) was known to Keystone prior to disclosure thereof to Keystone by ABC as evidenced by written records; or

c) is disclosed to Keystone by a third party under no obligation of confidentiality to ABC and without violation of this Agreement by Keystone.

Keystone agrees to hold in confidence all confidential information and not disclose such information to any other party without the written consent of ABC, and to refrain from making use of the information for its own benefit. Keystone agrees to disclose said information only to Keystone's accountant and attorney and agrees to return all such information immediately following the decision as to whether or not to enter this potential joint venture agreement.

This Agreement shall expire two years from the effective date of this Agreement and Keystone shall thereafter have no obligation of confidentiality with respect to any confidential information.

Keystone Inc.	ABC Corporation
By its President, Scott S. Burton	By its President, Nathan Northrop

Second-Chair Concept

One of the reasons for considering sharing the profits and responsibilities with another company is that, without the joint-venture approach, one company by itself might not be able to quality for the job. In some cases, this may be because one company lacks the equipment or the expertise to handle it. In other cases, it might simply be that one company has not and cannot qualify under the state's qualification statutes, many of which require residency for a certain period of time. If the latter is the reason, then it is like the attorney who gets permission from the court to participate in a particular case, even though she is from out of state and not a member of the local bar. The court will usually entertain this permission providing that local counsel sit in the "second chair." This is primarily to ensure that the time of the court is not wasted because trial counsel is unfamiliar with some of the local court procedures.

Preparation to Define the Relationship

All businesspeople should understand that contracts are not meant for the ill-intentioned. As discussed in other chapters, contracts are designed to resolve ambiguity and to override bad memory. If you are dealing with someone who has larceny in their heart, you may be sure that they're "gonna getcha!" But making sure that both parties agree on the same definition of a word or a phrase is always a good way to prepare a contract between most people with good intentions. If a definition is agreed on at the outset of a relationship, it is likely that the same definition will prevail at a later time.

> Remember that all contracts are designed to protect against ambiguity and bad memory.

Watch Out for the Small Print

When you're entering such an agreement, make sure you understand the meaning of the words—what they mean when they're first written, and what they may mean months or even years from now.

The Small Print Is Unimportant . . . Not!

Very often you will have someone say to you that the writing on the reverse side of a contract (sometimes recognizable by the fact that it's printed in yellow on pink paper) is unimportant. Sometimes they will refer to it as merely "the standard contract." Keep in mind that there are no "standard" contracts. The mere fact that someone calls it standard doesn't make it so. And if it were unimportant, why would they pay an attorney to draft it in the first place?! If it's there, it's important! And if you can't read it because it's too small, or if you can't understand it because the language is too obtuse, it may actually have a deceptive purpose. If you fail to read it, you'll be deceiving yourself.

The Small Print

Keep a magnifying glass handy to read most of these contracts. The print may very well be in eight-point type. Your Uncle Cy or Aunt Anne with poor eyesight at age 88 would never be able to read it, and even those hawks with 20–20 will have their problems. The rationale is that it's very small so it won't take up too many pages. After all, a lot of pages would be intimidating! In either case, don't be deceived. It was obviously designed for a purpose. Just make sure it doesn't conflict with the short- and long-term goals you have in mind.

Don't Forget the Content

What you want today is usually framed fairly well in most contracts between the parties, because each party understands what the short-term goals are. What you may want tomorrow is often left to be decided at a later date. Remember that language has to be crafted to handle circumstances that may change, and circumstances change all the time. Try to envision what kind of a business environment might prevail as things change. Try to use flexible language that can be adjusted in accordance with change. Remember that the Constitution was drafted a couple of hundred years ago and, aside from some singular interpretations by a clever few, the basics of this "contract" have endured fairly well. You will hardly be expected to draft a Constitution every time you prepare a written contract, but it wouldn't hurt to speak to your professional and try to anticipate the kind of framework that will accommodate a change in circumstances.

Collateral Elements

Even though the basic context of a contract constitutes the bulk of its language, keep in mind that most companies use the contract for a variety of collateral elements as well. Some speak to the issue of warranties and make it clear that any one of a variety of missteps, inadvertent or intentional, will void any warranty. Others speak to the issue of service contracts. Without looking carefully, you might not find out that the service aspects of your contract are good only for a certain period of time, after which the cost of service jumps

> Remember, there is no such thing as a standard contract when the contract elements are to be negotiated.

up dramatically. Still others will be relevant to penalties and surcharges, none of which will have been discussed between you and the person responsible for getting you to enter into the contract. For the most part, the best advice would be to speak to your professional and build that cost into the cost of the relationship. You will never be sorry!

The Subcontracting Element

More often than not, the two parties entering into a joint venture are not equal in terms of either responsibility or allocation of profit. In most cases, there is a primary party and a secondary party. The primary party is usually responsible for the entirety of the project, and the secondary party is usually responsible for a part of the project. You can compare this to the building of a house where there is a general contractor responsible for the finished project, ready for move-in, and a variety of secondary parties responsible for individual aspects such as plumbing, electricity, and the like. Whichever role your company plays in these scenarios, be sure that the language of the agreement contains requirements that you feel are within the parameters of your capabilities: personnel, equipment, and time availability. And then, make sure that the profit involved is commensurate with your normal margins and profit requirements.

The Strategic Alliance

If there is any difference between a joint venture and a strategic alliance, it is probably in the formality of the first, a written contract, and the informality of the second. When two companies recognize that each has something to gain by working together, buying from or selling to the other for example, then the business relationship has a reason for being. In most of these cases, there is no need for a written contract because things such as purchase orders based on price sheets are likely to eliminate the need for a more formal and all-encompassing written document. On the other hand, if one party is going to invest in additional inventory, equipment, or personnel, a written contract would be warranted. Similar situations would include exclusivity in buying or selling product. Again, there is nothing sacrosanct about either designation and you can switch them around as you choose. The important thing is to make sure that the appropriate documentation is prepared if the circumstances of the relationship appear to require such protection.

The Possibility of Acquisition or Merger

It is very interesting that, in many cases, the presence of synergy can lead to a merger of two companies or the acquisition of one by the other. As companies work together, just as in the relationship of the two architects mentioned above, the dream of accelerated growth can become a reality for both of them. The recognition that the two working together can accomplish much more than the aggregate of each company's solo success often leads to discussions not anticipated when the companies first met. Although this possibility deserves serious attention, be careful that, even with two companies as opposed to two individuals, the goals and expectations of both parties are in sync.

Worksheet Questions

1. How would you define synergy?

2. Can two people or two companies work together without forming a legal partnership?

3. Why are time lines so important in a joint venture?

4. Why is a nondisclosure or confidentiality agreement necessary when creating a joint venture?

5. Why is it important to maintain the security of all information disclosed?

---

6. What are the basic elements that need to be included in such an agreement?

7. What are the two things that a contract is designed to protect against?

8. Is there such a thing as a standard contract?

9. Why is it important to examine the short- and long-term goals and expectations of your relationship before executing an agreement?

10. Why is a merger or acquisition the possible result of a joint venture project?

11. What is the nondisclosure designed to protect against?

CHAPTER 13

Implicit
Partnerships
The Franchise

The Inequality of a
"Partnership Relationship"

When Jeff Bernstein entered into the franchise relationship, it was with all the optimism, energy, and goodwill required of any partnership. The after-market automobile components that he was selling were of high quality, and the franchise organization was small but appeared to be well-tuned. His personal relationship with the CEO was built on trust and confidence.

For the first year, all expectations appeared to be fulfilled. The question of the franchisor spending as much time with its company stores as with its franchised stores was of some concern but didn't appear to be a problem in the manufacture, delivery, and quality of essential merchandise. The business model for the franchised operations seemed to be well within the proper parameters for a profitable business.

The problem started with a twofold situation. The first evidence of a problem was failure to deliver the appropriate inventory to the stores. The second was that there was a lot of conversation about the price of component parts going up . . . and up . . . and up. By the time this problem trickled down to the franchise operation, the price of goods was so much higher than the original price structure that the business model was hardly viable.

It reached a point where the franchisees decided to source the parts themselves in the hope of bringing their business model back to a money-making position. Their franchise contract prevented them from seeking other sources without the express permission of the franchisor. When inventory was, once again, delivered, the prices were significantly higher than the original price structure. The worst part of the problem was that, in addition to the royalty paid to the franchisor, the franchise agreement also gave the franchisor the right to mark up the inventory before delivery to the franchisees . . . and they were not obliged to disclose the amount of the markup. This obviously led to additional distrust between the parties.

The reasons behind this franchisor attitude are unclear. The rumblings from various sources suggested that the company was having money problems that resulted in the executives soliciting investment from outside sources. And this appeared to be the core of the problem. Time was diverted from the needs of the franchisees.

The basic franchise concept and any success it may generate is predicated on the relationship between the parties. If the franchisees are successful, that success will invariably benefit the franchisor. The problem is that in the early days of a franchise operation, the money required for proper supervision of the franchisees is always more than the money that the franchisees contribute by franchise fee and royalty payments. If the franchisor can weather this early storm period, success is usually within reach. If franchisors haven't prepared for this situation, they will invariably try to increase their own margins (note the markup on inventory described above), which of course deviates from the business model originally set up to sell the franchise. The next stage is usually to look for investment dollars. And investors are generally interested in protecting their investment and getting an appropriate return on that investment even at the expense of the long-term success of a franchise operation.

The outcome is not unexpected. With the deterioration of the franchise business model, the franchisees begin having trouble achieving success. Then they started having trouble even surviving. They began to look around for alternatives. The passive among such a franchisee group will often close their businesses because they no longer have the money to subsidize the business. The bolder among them might attempt to band together in a more aggressive attempt at negotiating. Failing that, they will seek legal advice and examine the possibility of litigation. Whichever route they choose, the failure of the system is the obvious end result.

Closing the Business

The problem with closing the business is that the lost dollars don't stop at the loss of the original investment. The franchisee is usually signed to a relatively long lease, having anticipated a successful venture with the franchise. This lease commitment, often in the realm of hundreds of thousands of dollars, doesn't just go away. Remember, a $5,000-per-month rental on a five-year lease equals an obligation of $300,000. The franchisee has invariably signed this lease personally, or has guaranteed it personally, because his or her fledgling corporation's signature is rarely sufficient assurance to satisfy a lessor.

Jeff's situation was a mirror image of all the negative aspects described above. In fact, it was even worse. Jeff's optimism about the industry, of which this franchise was a part, inspired him to invest in four franchise operations in two different states. As he closed each location, he had to deal with the landlords with whom he had signed long-term leases.

❑ ❑ ❑

- Do you think Jeff should join with other franchisees to sue the franchisor?
- Do you think Jeff could have avoided this disaster in any way?
- Do you think Jeff should have read the franchise contract with a professional looking over his shoulder?
- Does this suggest that buying a franchise before the franchisor becomes financially stable is a bad idea?

Perhaps the most important and least respected aspects of partnerships are the ones that don't stand out in the legal definition. They include some relationships that pretend to be "absolutely not a partnership," as well as those that don't address the question at all. The ones that don't address the question are as simple as the spousal or "significant other" relationship where the investment capital as well as the spending of the profit involve more people than just the entrepreneur. The absolutely-not-a-partnership situation is exemplified in the franchise relationship, where the franchisor makes it very clear that the franchisee is not a partner, an agent, or a fiduciary of any kind. This deserves some immediate reflection. Take a look at the basic language.

"In all matters, you are an independent contractor. Nothing in this franchise agreement nor in the franchise relationship constitutes you as our partner, our agent, or our joint venturer. Neither party is liable for the debts, liabilities, taxes, duties, obligations, default, compliance, intentional acts, wages, negligence, error, or omissions of the other. Neither party shall act or have the authority to act as agent for the other and neither you nor we shall guarantee the obligations of the other nor in any way become obligated for the debts or expenses of the other . . . ." Is that clear?

Franchisor to the Table

The fact is that the profit of the franchise is split between the parties. How much closer can you come to a partnership?! But before you make any judgment, you ought to examine the relationship more closely. A partnership exists when two or more people or entities combine to form a for-profit business. Usually one partner brings something unique to the table and the other, presumably, brings experience or talent to augment the other's capabilities. In the case of a franchise, the franchisor (the franchise company) has the expertise and the experience of having been in the marketplace for some period of time. The company has usually created a format for the business, a product or service enhanced by client experience, and a reputation that has some advertising impetus. With these existing basics, the franchisee has a running start, so to speak, and brings the other important elements to the business partnership: the time, energy, and working capital so necessary to spark the new business.

The Profit Picture

If you want to create a scenario for a business partnership, the above elements certainly will fill the bill. The next aspect is that each partner anticipates sharing a part of the business's profits. In a franchise, instead of the partners sharing a percentage of the profit, the franchisor takes its percentage from the gross revenues generated by the business. The franchisee takes the profit that is left over after all expenses have been deducted from the revenues generated. The problem is that there will always be a percentage of gross revenues, but there might not be any profit after deducting expenses from revenues. If this doesn't seem fair, you need to examine the concept further.

Make sure you understand the profit picture for yourself and the franchisor.

A Franchise, for Good Reason

The people who become franchisees usually do so for good reason. They are, for the most part, unfamiliar with the particular trade or industry of which the franchise is a part. They often come to the franchisor because they lack experience in operating a business, any business. Sometimes, they bring a certain expertise to the table but may lack the ability to properly handle the financial paperwork, the knowledge to anticipate inventory obsolescence, the understanding of equipment needs, and the experience to deal with specifics of that nature. Whatever the lack of business experience, it is usually accommodated by a training program created by the franchisor. This allows the franchisee to become familiar with all aspects of running the business. It is a tremendous advantage to those who might otherwise fail for lack of general business acumen or adequate knowledge of the specifics of a given business.

This training represents a big portion of the franchise fee, which is the franchisor's first dip into the franchisee's pocket. This fee is usually for the initial setup and paperwork prepared by the franchisor. The amount is often predicated on the size and scope of the anticipated business. And sometimes, this upfront franchise fee is entirely arbitrary. Although this initial fee is often considered fair by franchisees because of the training, advice, and cautions given by the franchisor, it is the ongoing royalty that usually creates

> Discuss the franchise with other franchisees, as well as with your professional.

the problem in the relationship. After all, in most partnerships it is expected that all partners will continue to work at the business after the initial phase of setting up and preparing to function in the marketplace. The activities of the franchisor after setup are usually passive in nature—a continuous aggravation for the franchisee, whose very existence and survival depend on a constant stream of high-level activity.

Absence of an Exit Strategy

The reason for one of the keynotes of this book, "Diamonds are forever; partnerships are not," is that there is an understanding in all human relationships that "Change is the only constant." Each relationship depends on the ability of each person to adjust his or her expectations and goals. Sometimes, change is dynamically good, and sometimes it is dramatically bad. In either case, the partners in a relationship may not agree as to the next order of business, the next priority to be examined. And when the different opinions make it impossible to continue, there must be a way for one or the other of the partners to exit the business. The all-important focus of this exit strategy should be to preserve the integrity of the business. As in divorce courts, the judge will usually look to the well-being of the child rather than to the needs or expectations of either parent. Any good professional will advise that an exit strategy ought to be included in the original partnership papers to ensure that the business, under any circumstances, will be able to continue. *One of the problems with a franchise is that there is, essentially, no exit strategy for the franchisee.*

The Problem of the Franchise Contract

In the event that the franchisee and the franchisor have a disagreement of any kind, there is virtually no exit strategy for the franchisee. The franchisor may terminate the contract and the relationship in the event that there is any default on the part of the franchisee with respect to any of his or her obligations. The franchisee has no such option because the franchisor is essentially under no obligation to perform any specific activity. In the early days of franchising, the franchisor was under a variety of obligations to help the franchisee in a myriad of ways. As time exposed litigation as the only viable franchisee strategy for exiting the relationship, the new franchise documents appeared with fewer and fewer obligations on the part of the franchisor. In current documents, there are virtually no obligations at all.

> Make sure you understand what kind of help the franchisor is obliged to provide.

After the Dance Is Over

Most franchise agreements today include the franchisor's prerogative of taking over the leased premises, the telephone number, and the home web site of the franchisee if the franchise contract is terminated. They also forbid the franchisee from pursuing any aspect of the business that the franchisor considers competitive in any way. Take a look at some language from an actual contract.

> Upon termination or expiration of this Franchise Agreement for any reason . . . for a period of three years . . . neither you, nor your family, nor any of your members, owners, partners, managers, officers, or directors . . . shall directly or indirectly participate as an owner, operator, shareholder, director, partner, consultant, agent, employee, advisor, officer, lessor, lessee, or franchisee, or serve in any other capacity whatsoever or have any interest in or assist any person or entity in any business, firm, entity, partnership, or company engaged in the sale or offering of products or services or using a business format which is the same as or similar to ours or the system within the territory allocated or within ten miles of the territory of any other franchisee's or company-owned store's territory or business operation.

Although this quote has been shortened to some degree, it's easy to see that any exit strategy by the franchisee, and his or her ability to continue in the same or a similar business, has been completely abrogated by this kind of language.

And, Just in Case . . .

The franchisor has even anticipated the possibility that a court might find this to be unenforceable, as it obviously prevents the franchisee from pursuing perhaps the only business with which he or she may be familiar. So, just in case, they've included the following language:

> In the event these post-term restrictions are found to be unenforceable, the franchisee shall be obliged for a period of no less than three years, to pay a fee of one-half of the royalties and advertising fees which would be payable if the business operated by the former franchisee was still a franchise.

How about that?!

The Franchisor's Extra Margin of Profit

As if this weren't enough, you might also note the language that allows the franchisor to make a profit on any goods that it has manufactured for the benefit of the franchise system for delivery to the franchisees. Sometimes the product developed by the franchisor and sold at market by the franchisee is of such a proprietary nature that its protection is of extremely high priority. The pancake batter by a national chain of restaurants and the formula for a cola drink by an international manufacturer are just two examples. Unfortunately, the concept has been developed beyond all logic. Such protection is now guaranteed by virtue of the language in a franchise contract and precludes the possibility of examining other sources of components or finished product without the specific permission of the franchisor. And it makes little difference whether the product or service has any unique or special qualities deserving of protection or not. It merely represents another method by which the franchisor can enjoy a profit without worrying about whether the individual franchise operation shows a profit or not.

Closely examine the alternatives available to you, if any, when the franchise contract expires or is terminated. Examine all potential exit strategies.

Don't Forget the Good Things

Lest you lose sight of the franchise advantage in this nonpartnership situation, make sure to do an analysis of the differences not only between a franchise and a nonfranchise opportunity, but also between two franchises in the same industry. Keep in mind that you must receive a disclosure document about the franchise before any franchisor can have you sign agreements or take money from you. Note the language involved (capitalization is mandated by the government for every disclosure document):

> Build a business plan for the franchise as well as for an independent alternative.

> THIS OFFERING CIRCULAR SUMMARIZES CERTAIN PROVISIONS OF THE FRANCHISE AGREEMENT AND OTHER INFORMATION IN PLAIN LANGUAGE. READ THIS OFFERING CIRCULAR AND ALL AGREEMENTS CAREFULLY.
>
> IF THE FRANCHISE CORPORATION OFFERS YOU A FRANCHISE, THE CORPORATION MUST PROVIDE THIS OFFERING CIRCULAR TO YOU BY THE EARLIEST OF:
>
> - THE FIRST PERSONAL MEETING TO DISCUSS OUR FRANCHISE, OR
> - TEN BUSINESS DAYS BEFORE THE SIGNING OF A BINDING AGREEMENT, OR
> - TEN BUSINESS DAYS BEFORE ANY PAYMENT TO THE FRANCHISE CORPORATION.
>
> YOU MUST ALSO RECEIVE A FRANCHISE AGREEMENT CONTAINING ALL MATERIAL TERMS AT LEAST FIVE BUSINESS DAYS BEFORE YOU SIGN ANY FRANCHISE AGREEMENT.
>
> IF THE FRANCHISE CORPORATION DOES NOT DELIVER THIS OFFERING CIRCULAR ON TIME, OR IF IT CONTAINS A FALSE OR MISLEADING STATEMENT, OR A MATERIAL OMISSION, A VIOLATION OF FEDERAL AND

STATE LAW MAY HAVE OCCURRED, AND SHOULD BE REPORTED TO THE FEDERAL TRADE COMMISSION, WASHINGTON, DC 20580, AND TO THE APPROPRIATE STATE REGULATING AGENCY LISTED IN EXHIBIT "G."

I have received a Uniform Franchise Offering Circular dated June 5, 2006. This offering circular included the following exhibits:

- Franchise Agreement and Its Exhibits
- Noncompetition–Nondisclosure Agreement
- Required Purchases from Franchisor
- Financial Statements
- List of Agencies/Agents for Service of Process
- List of Affiliate-Owned Stores
- List of State Agencies responsible for Franchise Disclosure and Registration Laws
- Landlord's Consent to Assignment
- Table of Contents for Policies and Procedures Manual
- List of Franchisees
- Receipt
- Date   Franchisee

TWO COPIES OF THIS RECEIPT HAVE BEEN PLACED AT THE END OF THE ENTIRE OFFERING CIRCULAR PACKET. PLEASE SIGN BOTH OF THESE AND TAKE ONE FOR YOUR RECORDS.

This is the law. Also keep in mind that, at the back of these disclosure documents is a list of existing franchisees, along with their telephone numbers. The best advice anyone can receive relative to the possible acquisition of a franchise is to "Ask the person who owns one."

Inability to Compete

When you're finished with your franchise contract, even if not terminated (i.e., the contract merely expires), if there is a proper noncompete, you're essentially out of business. As you examine the alternative of buying a franchise or starting the same kind of business on your own, the question at the outset should be: Can you put something together that would be comparable, that would not violate any of the franchisor's copyrights, trademarks, etc., and that would not need the already existing franchise advertising in order to survive?

Once you order their disclosure document, you may have another problem. Be careful! You may have to sign a nondisclosure document along with the disclosure. This may also prevent you from entering that particular business, or at least be a serious deterrent. Franchising can be perfect for the right people for the right reasons. It really requires a thorough comparative analysis. See your professional to be sure that you're factoring in all the right elements.

The Litigation Alternative

Although there are many litigation attorneys who would look at such a case optimistically (obviously depending on the specific circumstances), any legal action will cost a franchisee or franchisee group many thousands of dollars to prosecute, with only a small percentage of them being successful. The franchisor has, over the years, tempered the franchise agreements to such an extent that their actual obligations to the franchisees are extremely limited. Watch out for advice that suggests otherwise.

What Is the Answer?

The answer is obvious. Whenever you are considering the purchase of a franchise opportunity, be sure to get the appropriate professional advice before making your commitment. Your "due diligence" needs to be much more sophisticated than what the average businessperson might think. Remember the standard caveat used by the International Franchise Association: "Investigate before investing."

This story is based on the experience of more than one franchise organization and is not meant to represent any single franchise business.

Worksheet Questions

1. Why is the franchise relationship not considered a partnership?

2. Do you know the source or sources of the franchisor's income?

3. What does the franchisee get in return for the initial franchise fee?

4. What is the franchisee expected to bring to the working relationship?

5. What are some of the reasons for an entrepreneur to buy a franchise?

6. What are some of the reasons for an entrepreneur not to buy a franchise?

7. What kind of exit strategy is available to the franchisee?

8. What kind of "post termination, post expiration" noncompete language is in the franchise agreement?

9. What is the best thing to do before making a commitment to buy a franchise?

10. What kind of professional should you discuss this with before making up your mind?

CHAPTER 14

Protecting Proprietary Information

Noncompete Clauses

Protecting Proprietary Information under the Law

In the case of Marty's Consumer Adjustment Service, Marty McArthur was careful to explain to all new employees that the methods that the employees would be learning during their training period were proprietary. He explained that it took him years to develop this system, spending long hours and, frankly, wasting many hours trying to develop the right system. As a result, Marty made it very clear that this "information system" belonged to the company, and was protected from any of it being used by employees, either for themselves or for a competitor. This warning was put in writing and included in every employee contract. The employees didn't have to sign this contract but if they did, they agreed to abide by its terms as part of their employment. To ensure that this was taken seriously, Marty tried to prevent any employee from having access to all the information and kept his departments independent of each other for that purpose. In many businesses, this is difficult, because the employees need to know the entire system in order to be effective. However, it is important to do everything you can to protect your information system. If you don't try to protect this information yourself, the court will wonder why it should take on the responsibility you neglected.

Did It Work?

Unfortunately, three employees decided to create a competitive company by using Marty's information system after becoming quite familiar with all its details and nuances. Marty brought a legal action to stop them from continuing in that business. What action do you think the court took in this situation?

The company, suing to protect its proprietary information, retained a business expert to testify on its behalf relative to what it did to protect the information, and what the measure of damages ought to be. The relevant portion of the expert's affidavit will explain the company's position:

> It is my opinion that the methods, systems, and techniques utilized by Plaintiff in its marketing and production functions are highly developed, systematized, and detailed, and have evolved and been developed to a degree which allows Plaintiff to identify, access, and service its market in a distinct and profitable manner. Plaintiff has taken care to develop and secure execution by its employees of employment agreements seeking to advise the employees of the value of Plaintiff's information and seeking to protect that information.
>
> Accordingly, this is not a case in which a party seeks court protection of information when it has failed itself to take reasonable protective actions. While it is true that any case involves the difference between the normal employee reservoir of intellectual information developed during time spent in a particular trade industry and the specific information acquired during tenure with a specific company and its training, I believe that this client's information falls outside the parameters of the "employee intellectual reservoir." My reason is based primarily on the time it takes for anyone to

become proficient in the use of the marketing and product systems, and the ongoing training involved in getting the employee to that level of sophistication.

The information, systems, and techniques provide Plaintiff an opportunity for substantial competitive advantage. As a result, the systems, methods, and techniques developed and utilized by Plaintiff have a significant value in the marketplace and could be licensed to others for valuable consideration. Just as a franchise company licenses its conceptual and marketing knowledge for a fee, even though no single portion may actually be protectable per se, this totality of concept is the foundation of a new business. I believe we have that same situation in the present case. As with any franchise, there is a learning/teaching aspect to the business. The teaching is initially designed to put the employee into play, so to speak, but a real understanding of the business comes only through constant training and retraining over a period of certainly no less than six (6) months. This information is the core of Plaintiff's business. It is also significant that the employees cannot be totally separated in terms of management vs. labor or one department vs. another. If this could be done, the protective aspect of the materials would be easier to effect. Unfortunately, in this business, employees need to know practically all aspects of the business before the employee can function properly.

The information, systems, and techniques utilized by Plaintiff are analogous to the aggregate of information provided in a franchise package. Most franchises do not have any special or secret information that can be protected per se through copyright, trademarks, trade secrets, or patents. However, in the aggregate, this information has been developed over a substantial period of time and at a cost commensurate with that time. This is what a franchise candidate enjoys when he or she pays the franchise fee and a continuing royalty on sales. It is a combination of both positive and negative information, valuable as much for what it tells the owner not to do as for what it should do to run an efficient and profitable business.

It is also my opinion that a significant amount of effort, time, and money would be required to duplicate Plaintiff's methods, systems, and techniques as utilized. So far as the question of "damages" is concerned, I would continue to compare this to the value of the core franchise elements entitled to protection under the law.

❑ ❑ ❑

- If you were the judge sitting on this case, what would your opinion be?
- Do you think the consultant's explanation as to the value of the information is strong enough?
- What would be your counter argument?

The question of "enforcement" against "employees" is conjectural in many states. Some states have right-to-work laws that severely limit a company's ability to prevent employees from pursuing the only business or trade with which they are familiar. And this is true even when they learned all of what they know from the firm they are leaving. On the other hand, the law does not look so warmly at a person who held an equity position in a company and then left to pursue a competitive position. Part of the reason for this is that a person in management usually has access to the entire spectrum of proprietary information and methodologies of the company. Employees normally have access to information about those areas for which they are responsible but are not privy to the totality of the company's concepts. In addition, the partner or other part-owner understands the nature of the proprietary information and is usually aware that it is to be protected against any competition.

Can You Really Protect Against Disclosure?

The problem of employee retention has attained higher visibility than usual in today's intellectual melting pot. A good idea, years ago, was usually the beginning of a long journey. It involved accessing raw material, developing a cost-effective manufacturing process, understanding the marketplace to make an assessment as to the best advertising approach, and hiring the most appropriate people for an aggressive foray into the business marketplace. In today's fast-moving, internet marketplace, a good idea might be minutes away from implementation and profit. One of the problems with this accelerated growth picture is the fact that the idea, taken by a competitor, could find its way into the marketplace before a second management conference is even called to assess its potential. And what happens when one of the management team decides to move across the street to a competitor, idea in pocket?

Can You Stop an Employee from "Crossing the Street"?

Many employees leave their company because of personal conflict with peers or supervisors. Some leave because they have been offered a better opportunity for advancement or a substantial increase in pay. But what happens when the offer for opportunity or pay is predicated not on the quality of the individual but rather on the quality of his or her information? Should it make a difference? If so, what kind of a difference should it make? This is sometimes referred to as "corporate espionage."

> Be careful to properly assess the equation between disclosure to develop loyalty and disclosure that would be inimical to the best interests of your company.

You might have all your employees sign a nondisclosure, an agreement not to disclose information of a confidential nature in the event they leave the company for any reason. But the question remains: What, exactly, is confidential information? There is a controversial legal theory known as "inevitable disclosure," which maintains that an employee working in the same industrial environment will disclose, even if unintentionally, whatever is in his or her intellectual toolbox. In other words, ethics notwithstanding, the mere use of one's experience and general knowledge in the field would constitute disclosure. If this is true and this presumption is accepted in the courts, the result would be that you wouldn't even have to prove "intent"; all you'd have to show is that the employee "crossed the street." This, of course, flies in the face of the idea that a company shouldn't be able to prevent an ex-employee from making a living. After all, if someone has been an engineer for 20 years, it wouldn't be fair to expect him or her to get a job at a fast-food chain after leaving their company.

Industrial Espionage and the Subtler Problem

But what happens when a competitor is so determined to learn the trade secrets of a company, or is so desperate for the customer list of a successful

<blockquote>Make sure you give the appropriate dignity to the proprietary information you seek to protect.</blockquote>

competitor, that they pay your employee to either disclose the information or cross the street for a new job? The first of these, of course, is in the category of industrial espionage and is easier to recognize and deal with. The second of these is more difficult to define.

The Question of Enforcement

Whether or not you can protect against any such disclosure depends very much on the law of the particular jurisdiction in which you live, the discretionary position of the court regarding the question of intent, and your ability to show the significant value of the information as well as the nature and extent of your damages. All of the above represent a long, tedious road at best. And make no mistake about it: this road also represents a very expensive ride! It is not one to be taken lightly.

The Real Answers

There are two ways to protect against such a problem. The first is to give the information you want to protect the proper dignity. It should be made available only to key employees on a need-to-know basis. Certainly, each component of a project can be isolated from other parts, which means that the employees working on either will not necessarily be aware of the other. Yet it is also true that certain employees, of necessity, must know all the information in order to put the components together for the finished product. Whenever the information becomes significantly valuable, it should be protected as best it can. This is not always easy and is usually not foolproof.

The best answer is to incentivize the employees by creating the most advantageous retention plan the company can handle. Being "penny wise and pound foolish" is clearly contrary to the best interests of management in the long term. You've got to make the employees feel that the company they work for is *theirs*; that giving information to the competition is not in their best interests. But don't forget the key! Words, slogans, and promises are easy to make, easy to break, and, more often than not, will fall on deaf ears. If your intention is to protect and benefit your company and you recognize the dynamic vulnerability of disclosure, put your game plan together NOW! Tomorrow's lawsuit could have been avoided by action taken yesterday. Do it today!

What the Court Looks For

In order to enforce a noncompete against either an employee or an equity partner, the company must have given sufficient protection to the proprietary information to suggest that it considers such information to be private, valuable, and in need of protection. Many courts have indicated that they would not enforce such protection because the company did not devote sufficient resources to protecting it themselves. They failed to make an attempt to keep some things private and inaccessible to all employees except those whose jobs depend on that knowledge. Some courts put it this way: "Why should we enforce this protection when the company didn't give it the appropriate dignity themselves?"

Is the Recovery Merely in Terms of Dollars?

Most of this kind of litigation is brought after the fact. It is difficult for a court, even if it is of the belief that this misappropriation of information was improper, to actually stop a company from doing business. This is especially true considering that the time to "get to court" usually means that the new company has already been in business for some appreciable period of time. In such a case, the court must determine the extent of damages, in dollar terms, that would fairly compensate the original business for the tortious conduct committed by the exiting partner or employee. As noted previously, the first judgments by the court will address the questions of "Did the company try to protect the information adequately?" and "Is the information deserving of protection in the first place?"

Sharing Financial Information Generally

Although public companies are under the obligation to share their complete financial information with the general public by preparing annual and quarterly financial statements, the private sector, the closed corporation, is under no such obligation.

Sharing with Your Banker, Your Lawyer, Your Accountant

There are certain people with whom you must share this information for a variety of reasons. The bank will certainly want to review your financials to be

> The sharing of information with professionals and institutions should always be carefully assessed and monitored.

sure that their loan to you, or your line of credit, or your anticipated relationship, will have some stability. Your accountant is the reservoir of this information, or should be, in order to ensure that your activities are within the parameters of good record-keeping. Your lawyer should usually be apprised of your financial condition at least periodically, because without the appropriate advice, automatic renewal of the lease or changes in your contract relationships could be problematic.

Selling the Business

When a buyer is interested in acquiring a business, he or she will certainly want to see the financial information available about that company. The question is: To what information is the buyer entitled? And, perhaps even more important: When should that information be made available? There is a time sequence involved in the selling of a business. Certainly, a potential buyer should see the basic financial information about the business once the seller is satisfied that the buyer is serious and qualified. Even then, however, the amount of information should be limited to the amount sufficient to warrant further conversation. Information about customer lists and specific line-items should be avoided. To be sure you are not "giving away the store," be sure to discuss this with your professional.

Sharing Information with Your Vendors

Vendors want to know that they are dealing with healthy companies. The amount of information available to them should be limited to that purpose.

Knowing too much about the inner workings of your business, particularly in hard times, could cause them to question your ability to make timely payments and raise other questions of quantity purchases, collection procedures, and the like. Be careful about filling out these credit applications. Honesty is not antithetical to limited disclosure.

Protecting Financial Information from Your Competitors

One of the best ways to make judgments about your approach to the competitive marketplace is to know what your competitors are doing. Not only is it necessary for a new business to check price comparisons, it is also helpful to know what specials the competition is offering and what items they have ordered more or less for the coming season. This is the kind of information that they are looking for from you as well. It's fair game in the business community. The information that you want kept private is that which has to do with your financial condition. This should be kept close to the vest. If you're going to share financial information with a competitor, make sure that the sharing is equal and that you're not putting yourself in an equivocal position.

Worksheet Questions

1. What is the biggest danger when a partner decides to leave and start a business in competition with your own?

2. Do you think it's any different when an employee starts the competing business?

3. Do you think it's any different in the mind of the court whether your competitor is a former partner or an employee?

4. Do you think that these two situations should be handled differently?

5. Can you really protect your proprietary information against disclosure?

---

6. How effective is a nondisclosure agreement?

7. What does it mean to give your proprietary information "the proper dignity"?

8. What is the most practical way to protect your company from employee disclosures?

9. Do you think the expert's affidavit is substantial enough to convince a court?

10. Why is it necessary to share vital information with certain people and institutions?

11. Do you think it's ethical protocol to seek out proprietary information about your competitors?

12. How can you protect your proprietary information when creating a joint venture or strategic alliance with a competitor?

13. What kind of information should be protected at any cost?

CHAPTER 15

Building a Business with or without Partners

Avoiding the Great Deceptions
The Shoe Shop and the Print Shop

Sam Arbicki followed in his father's footsteps by taking over control of a small but successful shoe repair business. Having learned the business under his father's tutelage, Sam understood the nuances of the business. He opened and operated several additional stores and caught the attention of some investors who examined the profitability of the businesses and recognized the concept as a good franchise opportunity. The prospect of accelerated growth excited Sam even though the additional investment meant that he would have to give up control in the larger operation. His attitude was that he would have a smaller piece of a bigger pie and that seemed like a good opportunity.

The new investors, with 51 percent of the new business, created a franchise operation that, although successful, needed much more money to maintain the supervisory personnel and the marketing impetus to sustain its growth in the marketplace. It was decided that the company would create an IPO, an initial public offering, which would generate the big dollars necessary for growth of the franchise. The IPO offering put out 44 percent of the company's equity to the public. Sam gave up most of his equity position, retaining 5 percent of the bigger business. Again, his philosophy prevailed: Better to have a small piece of a big business than a big piece of a small business.

The IPO, which sells shares of a company to outsiders in the national marketplace, generated the additional capital needed and attracted bigger names with more corporate experience. The theory was that these experienced people would be better administrators than those who understood the small-business concepts but who had little experience with "the big picture." Within two years, after spending money that they had not earned themselves, these "experienced administrators" left the company and the company declared bankruptcy. Sam's equity position in the company had gone from 100 percent to 49 percent to 5 percent to 0! Sam remained philosophical: "It was a heckofa ride and I learned a great deal about business, about 'big shots,' and about myself."

After the bankruptcy, Sam opened another shop. When asked about the future, he said: "I now have 100 percent of a small business. I have no one looking over my shoulder. I make a good living without having to report to others. This is the way I like it."

Avoiding the Great Deception

Bill Leverall owned a printing business that continued to grow as he put his best energies into the company. Because of equipment innovations in the industry, it was suggested to Bill that he could create a franchise operation out of his business. Being a somewhat conservative entrepreneur, Bill was skeptical but continued to examine the prospect during the following years. He finally decided that the opportunity made sense. He started conservatively by opening a small shop with his own people. After opening a few others, he realized that the concept indeed made sense and that each shop could stand on its own and provide a solid profit for an owner. He started a franchise operation by using his own funds and by doubling the responsibilities of his current employees, having each of them assume some supervisory capacity. Although this was clearly not a long-term answer, it provided Bill with a temporary solution instead of assembling an entirely new group of people to handle the franchise operation at this early stage.

The innovation in equipment convinced other companies to follow suit but Bill was one of the first in the franchise game and, over the next 15 years, grew the largest franchise system in the industry. Many others did the same and prospered as well. When Bill ultimately took his company public via an IPO, he converted his equity position to a multiple of his original investment.

Bill had taken a somewhat conservative approach to building a bigger business. It took a lot more time than Sam's adventure, but the proof is in the pudding. Would you have been willing to take Sam's gamble to shorten the road to success?

Opposite Sides of the Coin

The differences between the two ventures above make it clear that success and failure are merely two sides of the same coin. Each man had the opportunity to make good things happen. Sam had the bad fortune to affiliate with partners who had little concern for him, who were moved by greed, and who lacked the discipline to create a solid company out of a good idea. Bill, on the other hand, chose to use the people he trusted as partners, to form the basic cadre to establish his business model. He then chose to move conservatively toward the goal of creating a business that would work for others; in turn, it worked for him as well. Although Sam's partners were in the game strictly for money, Bill's partners, as well as Bill himself, were as concerned about the success of each individual franchise as they were about the system as a whole. They understood that the big picture of success could not be realized without the success of each of the small, individual, franchised shops. It even became well known that Bill himself had actually loaned money to a franchisee who was having trouble in the early days. This franchisee, by the way, turned his small business into

> Remember that investors in your business will have some influence over your decisions in the long term, especially concerning exit strategies.

a million-dollar operation. These stories present solid evidence for the venture capitalist conviction that it's better to invest in a solid management team with a weak product, than in a solid product with a weak management team. You can certainly see why. Picking your partners is a critical element in the design and building of a successful business. Truly, there is nothing that can replace trust in any such relationship!

The Next Question

The idea of working with a partner or partners is the main consideration of this book. And understanding the diverse lifestyles of each partner is the predicate for a successful partnership relationship. Along with this extraordinarily difficult task, one of the first questions that such a relationship will face is whether to build a business from the ground up or to buy a business that already exists. This question certainly warrants attention.

Better to Build or Buy a Business?

The advantage of building a business from scratch is that you can do the whole thing your own way. If it's a retail shop, you can envision the build-out, and then make it happen. If it's a service business, you can buy or lease the equipment you want and pick your own customer base and design your own marketing plan. These and other prerogatives of ownership are entirely in your hands. The problem is that after you've speculated on the benefit of these prerogatives, you not only have to get the job done but you've also got to start winning your customers, one at a time. This requires capital. And you must spend this capital before your cash flow starts to positively impact your bank account. Generally, you start from behind and gradually catch up before you can enjoy that positive profit at the end of the day.

Cash Flow Is the Key

On the other hand, if you examine your prospective industry and find a business already in existence, you have an alternative to building from scratch. You certainly should recognize other businesses in the field because, having researched your anticipated venture, you will have performed competitive analyses of all competition in the field. If you've not done this, you haven't started on the right foot. If you have, you are in a position to know the differentials involved in your prospective competition. The question is, are any of these businesses for sale? For one reason or another, these businesses may not be phenomenally profitable, but each of them will have a cash flow. It is your job to decide if any have enough potential for growth to make them viable as potential acquisitions.

> Remember that growing your company has some inherent dangers, including the question of cash flow, and usually requires additional working capital.

The Advantage to Acquisition

As you read the chapter on how to evaluate a business for purchase or sale, you will note that the key to success is that "the business must be able to buy itself." What this means is that the owner compensation as well as the purchase price must be paid from the profit of the business. If this can't happen, you should take a pass on the business. But if it can happen, you've got the makings of a potential success. After the purchase price is paid off, these dollars then drop into your pocket. You can see that buying a business can be dramatically different from creating a new one that may then be in competition with the one you could have bought. There are several variables involved in this potential scenario, such as the negotiating of a down payment, the length of time you should be paying the balance of the purchase price based on the risk involved in the industry, and the like. It may not be a bed of roses, but it's certainly worth a careful examination of the differentials by all partners.

Affiliation as an Alternative; the Unauthorized Franchise

There are further subtleties involved in establishing a business, including the possibility of creating a partnership with an existing business to take advantage of the customer base already established. This can come in many forms. A

Buying an existing business can often be less expensive and less problematic than building one from scratch.

franchise is one example of using the experience of an existing organization to enjoy the benefits of your own energies without wasting time on efforts that may be less than effective in the marketplace. Another approach might be to have someone take you and your partners under their wing, so to speak. Some companies will charge you for the privilege; others might invest their time in your business for a portion of the business: i.e., an equity position in the company. Be sure, however, that one of these scenarios is not contrary to existing franchise legislation. If you plan to use both the name and the marketing program of an existing brand, and you will be paying for it on an incremental basis after you've started the business, you may be in violation of franchise laws. And this is true even if the original organization doesn't think so.

Don't Forget about Joint Ventures and Strategic Alliances

Remember that these arrangements often lead to acquisition of one business by another. You might want to revisit Chapter 12, the one on joint ventures and strategic alliances.

After all, when two businesses find it profitable to utilize one another when neither could perform the job alone, the presumption is that this could be a long-term profitable relationship. The two management teams or the partners representing each business will invariably discuss whether the arrangement has the potential of becoming permanent. After acknowledging the positive synergy between the two companies, the next consideration is whether management of one can get along with the management team of the other. It's very much the same discussion that two partners may have at the beginning of any partnership arrangement.

The "Active" vs. the "Passive" Partner

There is a significant difference between an active and a passive partner. The active partner is a participant, and must be kept apprised of all decisions and directions of the company on an immediate basis. The passive partner, although not involved in the day-to-day activities, should be apprised on a periodic basis. This should include an assessment as to which successes have been achieved, which have not yet reached fruition, the time frame involved in the eventual achievement, and the anticipated time line for the fulfillment of the business's goals and expectations. In this way, the passive partner will get a sense of involvement without management answering questions that might inhibit the growth or direction of the company.

The Business Plan, Again

The business plan is designed to check the feasibility of a business, to establish the basics of its implementation, to convince a lender to create a line of credit, or to entice an investor to join the company. It is one of the earliest documents of any company's paper trail. The business plan also presents the easiest way to check on past performance, to see which investments were the most successful, which were the best costs against revenues, and which directions just didn't pan out. By reviewing and renewing your business plan once every six months or even once a year, all management people and all investors can make their own judgments as to the continuing viability of the company, the things the company should not do again, and those things that appear to be moving the company in the right direction. Do you think that Sam Arbicki was following a business plan? If not, do you think it might have helped? Do you think that Bill Leverall was following a business plan? You bet he was!

Entering a Partnership Relationship in Another Way

When you borrow money, you have the obligation to repay the loan, together with the appropriate interest. After payment is made, you no longer have any continuing obligation to the lender. When you take investment capital in return for a percentage of ownership in your company, you don't have to repay the money unless and until the company is in a position to do this. On the other hand, this investment will represent ownership in the business for the long term. The one thing that each entrepreneur is not anxious to forfeit is complete control over the business. The lender is not in a position to do this once the money has been repaid. The equity owner, who is essentially a partner, may be in a position to exercise some control over the direction of the company. Do you want this?

Big Pie or Little Pie?

When examining the question of investments, the age-old question invariably rears its head: Would you rather have a small piece of a large business or a big piece of a small business? Although there are many perspectives on this question, the answer usually leans toward the small piece of a big business. The reason for this is that most entrepreneurs dream of big profit and big profit is, more often than not, the result of big investment. After all, big investment allows for more qualified personnel, immediate purchase of equipment and inventory, as well as a marketing attack that can literally inundate your potential customer base and beat your competitors to the punch. The fact that a bigger company can also afford bigger salaries is another consideration of the entrepreneur whose dream is yet to become a reality. Is this where Sam made his biggest mistake?

What's Goin' On?

The passive partners in a business, even with the benefit of a periodic business plan and periodic meetings, will essentially be examining the company's affairs after the fact. Their input may be terribly important and create positive adjustments for the future. Unfortunately, although such input is essential to the maintenance and growth of the company, it is usually too late to take advantage of that advice for present-day activities. Active partners, on the other hand, need to be apprised much more often in order to offer advice that will impact the company's activities day to day. One partner, who may be in charge of all ordering, for example, is not likely to know all that he or she needs to know in order to fulfill the obligations of that office. Since things usually have a way of tying in, it is essential that all partners know what the others are doing in order to ensure that time frames and other expectations are being properly coordinated. This is one of the reasons why most management teams will have weekly meetings to avoid any problems. These meetings should not be for the purpose of second-guessing anyone. They should be geared to ensuring continuity and follow through.

Worksheet Questions

1. Why is it preferable, in some instances, to borrow money rather than to have someone invest in your company?

2. Why is it preferable, in other instances, to have someone invest in your company rather than to borrow from a lending institution?

3. What are some of the advantages of operating a small company?

4. Would you rather have 100 percent of a small successful business, or a much smaller percentage of a much larger company?

5. Do you think the question of keeping or losing control is an important factor?

6. Do you think it's wiser to build a business from scratch or to buy one?

7. Do you think that cash flow is an important part of this answer?

8. Do you think it's generally more expensive to buy a business than to build one?

9. What is the key consideration in buying an existing business?

10. Do you think that risk is important to factor in when evaluating a business to buy?

11. Do you think that a joint venture could be a good method of growth rather than acquisition?

12. What are the various uses of a business plan?

13. How can you use the business plan to do periodic comparative analyses of the business?

Putting It in Writing

Don't Neglect Your Paperwork

Rob and Sarah bought an old building that they renovated. Subsequently, they converted a portion of the building into an "outdoor store." Because there was additional space available, they decided to serve food and, despite their lack of experience, opened a small restaurant. They soon discovered that their lack of experience was leading to a lack of profit.

Some interested friends, who had limited restaurant experience, took over the operation of the restaurant. The arrangement was agreed to verbally and finalized with a handshake. No paperwork was prepared to define the legal aspects of the relationship. They merely agreed to split the profits after paying a minimal salary to each of the friends. But the friends did not operate the restaurant properly, and there was no profit. The restaurant was actually being subsidized by the outdoor store.

Rob and Sarah decided to terminate the relationship with their friends. It was actually a partnership, because the parties presented themselves to the community in that context, even though no paperwork had been created. Rob and Sarah then went back to operating the restaurant themselves. Whether it was their better management or merely the passage of time, they were able to put the restaurant right-side up. The restaurant became a success and started to make a profit.

When the "friends" found out about the profit, they sued Rob and Sarah for their alleged percentage of the profit. By not initiating the appropriate paperwork between them at the outset of their "restaurant relationship," the parties had unwittingly created a partnership—a general partnership.

Having been terminated as partners, did they have a right to any part of the profits?

If the friends had held themselves out as partners, with Rob and Sarah's permission or even with their mere tacit acknowledgement, could Rob and Sarah have claimed that the friends were actually employees and not entitled to any percentage of profits?

Since the case was settled out of court, these questions remain unanswered. It is quite likely, however, that a court could find for the friends because they went into the restaurant and gave it their best efforts as a result of the "arrangement" to which Rob and Sarah had agreed.

What might Rob and Sarah have done to avoid this problem?

The Definition of a Contract . . . Not for the Ill-Intentioned

Most businesspeople are under the erroneous belief that contracts are designed to protect against fraud, misrepresentations, and the like. Nothing could be further from the truth. In today's sophisticated business society, those people who have larceny in their hearts are "going to get you" regardless of any written words with a signature at the bottom. The fact of the matter is that contracts are really designed to compensate for two basic human frailties. The first problem is ambiguity. The contract will usually clarify language so that both parties acknowledge the meaning of phrases and concepts. The other problem is bad memory. It is not unusual for two people to remember an entirely different arrangement or agreement after some time passes. A written contract brings both people's memories back to the original discussion, clarifying any discrepancies in recollection.

> Be sure to seek professional advice before defining the partnership arrangement.

Operating Agreements and Bylaws

Whether you start your business with a simple partnership agreement or choose to seek the protection of a limited liability company (LLC) or corporation, you will need to set the record straight by developing the prerogatives and obligations of decision making, and establishing the protocols by which the business will be operated. Establishing these bylaws, or elements of an operating agreement, is mandatory and should include an exit strategy that sets basic goals and a course of action should a partner decide to leave the company. This is the time to seek the advice of your professionals. Arrangements for stock purchase or sale, for example, can have serious tax implications. Trying to take care of this kind of problem, after the fact, can be the cause of never-ending and never-healing wounds to the psyche as well as to the bank account. You should have a clear understanding of this subject before using language in your agreement that is unclear or detrimental to any of the partners.

Prerogatives and Obligations

In every business relationship there must be a method, established early on, by which decisions can be made on a daily, if not a minute-to-minute, basis. Without this protocol, a business can literally "stop" at times that would be inappropriate to the best interests of the company. This is a situation that all partners want to avoid. It is the fallibility of the human being that causes problems; it is the intellect of the human being that

> A contract is not designed for the ill-intentioned. It is to protect against confusion arising from ambiguity and bad memory.

It is important to define the prerogatives and obligations of the parties as well as the basic business protocols early in a partnership arrangement.

is designed to prevent this from happening. A good partnership will meet this challenge at the beginning.

You'll remember the adage, "Too many cooks spoil the broth." In a business context, you can't have a unanimous or even a majority decision on every action that the company takes. This would obviously be cumbersome, and would prevent the business from moving forward on a day-to-day basis.

The Partnership Game Plan

It is assumed that in every partnership relationship there is faith and confidence in the opinions and judgments of the partners. This assumption should automatically lead to an allocation of responsibilities among partners. Although it is not possible for one partner to abrogate all responsibility for certain decisions to another partner, it is certainly appropriate, if not necessary, for some allocations to be made. In any partnership, splitting job responsibilities results in a "doer" and a "watcher." As long as the watcher is not micromanaging or becoming a backseat driver, this balance can be very effective. One of the most dynamic of these responsibilities is understanding the cash flow, the cash reservoir, and the cash position of the company at all times. Although this subject is covered in Chapter 11, suffice to say that every partner has the responsibility of maintaining a clear and current understanding of these matters.

The Equipment Lease

One of the problems in developing these essential protocols is that when agreements are created during the early days of a partnership, the tendency is to accommodate those things of a high priority and to leave, for a later time, those things that seem less urgent. Unfortunately, it's very much like the company that is leasing expensive equipment. There are so many aspects to examine and negotiate about the initial terms relative to price, costs, warranties, and the like that the buyers (lessees) may overlook what will happen at the end of the lease.

Lease terms, relative to expensive equipment, can be quite different in each case. In some cases, for example, the lessee has the right, at the end of the lease, to purchase the equipment. The purchase price can be based on a variety of factors. The value of the equipment can be based on depreciation, the market value of the equipment at the time of purchase, or a one-dollar stipulation. It may even be predicated

> Equipment leases need to be carefully examined for the requirements at the end of the lease.

on the lessee using a specific amount as a down payment on a new piece of equipment as a replacement. By not looking at the residual value at the end of the lease, the buyer can be looking at a situation that may not be in the best interests of the company. It is worth the additional time to examine this with your professional.

What about Maintenance?

Another situation arises at the outset of a lease for substantial and expensive equipment, when the maintenance cost is usually factored in. This protection is a very important aspect of the purchase. At the end of the lease, when the lessee has the right to purchase the equipment, it must be kept in mind that the equipment is now considered used, and, as such, requires considerably higher maintenance costs than when the equipment was new. In fact, the cost of the maintenance contract alone will sometimes be the equivalent of the purchase price, the interest factor, and the maintenance cost of the original contract. Don't you think it would be appropriate to know this when you sign the original contract?

The Signature Is Important

Don't forget, when you sign as a partner in a partnership, all partners are then bound by that signature (jointly and severally) to the full dollar amount of the obligation. In addition, if the partnership has opted to create an entity such as a corporation or an LLC that will give each partner protection against long-term liabilities, such as equipment leases, you must be

> Be mindful of the difference between your corporate signature and your personal signature.

sure that you sign all documents properly or you will forfeit the protection. If you are a corporate officer, make sure that your corporate designation, such as vice president, is affixed to your name. If you fail to do this and sign only your name, you will lose the protection of the corporate entity and you can be held personally liable for the entire obligation.

What about the "Other" Lease?

With all the obligations inherent in the paperwork of a new business, none is more important than the premises lease for a retail business. The first thing that the new partnership should reflect on is the fact that $3,000-a-month rent on a five-year lease represents a long-term obligation to the partnership of $180,000. All partners should be aware of the substantial obligation to which they are affixing their signatures. And whether your business is successful or otherwise, this obligation doesn't go away.

Another aspect of the written lease is the "option to renew." Unfortunately, in some leases, this language is so ambiguous as to not really constitute an option to renew at all. The purpose of the option to renew is to create a set of parameters that will allow the partners to anticipate the future, and factor into its P&L all the costs against revenues necessary for the business to maintain its continuity. A real option to renew will set out the terms of the option period in specific detail, or it will say that the original terms will prevail with certain exceptions. If the option to renew merely says that the parties will have an option to renew but lacks any specific terms, this language may only give the lessee an opportunity to discuss the matter. In such a case, the lessee may be subjected to the lessor presenting entirely different terms than were contained in the original lease. As you can plainly see, this is hardly an option to renew at all.

The Informal Contract

In all business dealings, having documentation to memorialize the agreement of the parties is essential. In court proceedings, for example, where documentation is absent, the judge will have to make a decision based on the credibility of the parties. Any paperwork that was prepared contemporaneous with the incident in question will make that job easier for the court. It cannot be something that was prepared in anticipation of the court proceedings the night before the hearing because this would obviously be wrought with bias and singular memory. It must have been prepared for the purpose of the agreement at the time of the agreement. This is the most credible paperwork. When one partner is dealing with a vendor or a client, the other partner is subject to the first partner's memory. It is difficult to stand behind a bad memory. Always, always put the agreement in writing even in those cases where documentation is not called for in the relationship. Be sure to at least write a narrative or a letter to the other party. If this letter has a date and an appropriate signature, it will serve the court should the parties fail to agree.

Legal Approach

The best approach is to detail or outline the discussion and agreement, at the end of which you can write, "If I do not hear from you to the contrary in the next week, I will assume that the above is consistent with your understanding of our discussion." Judge Judy likes to have such recollections in writing. If the other party ends up disputing the material in the letter but failed to do so at the time of receipt, the court will want to know why. If the explanation is not credible or acceptable to the court, the letter will stand as the only and the best evidence. Keep this in mind.

Even for Employees

All partners recognize that in dealing with banks, investors, vendors, or clients, there is usually a written document between the parties. This can be a promissory note with the bank, a stock certificate with an investor, even a purchase order from a customer. This should suggest that, even with employees, there must be some sort of contract or agreement, even if just a letter, stating the basis of the relationship as well as certain cautions and obligations on the part of each party.

Equal Dignity for the Family

It is very interesting that in most family situations, all business arrangements are consummated by a hug or a handshake. This is even true of friends investing in a business. It is unfortunate, though, because time will usually create a slightly different memory of the agreement as circumstances may cause people to "need to have a different memory." The best way to ensure that the value of the family or friendship remains the highest priority is to document the new financial relationship, eliminating future problems of ambiguous language and bad memory. Why not give your family relationship the same dignity you would give to a stranger?

Worksheet Questions

1. Why is a contract not for people with bad intentions?

2. What is the purpose of an operating agreement between partners?

3. Why do protocols need to be developed at the beginning of a partnership?

4. Can one partner abrogate all responsibility by assigning a job to a partner?

5. What is the difference between a watcher and a doer in a partnership?

6. Why is cash flow a responsibility that cannot be assigned to a single partner?

7. What are the various alternatives to a purchase at the end of a lease term?

8. Why is it important to use the correct corporate signature?

9. What is the definition of "joint and several"?

10. What is the best way to ensure the validity of the option to renew a lease?

11. What is the best way to document an agreement when no paperwork is needed?

12. Why is it a good idea to have a written agreement from all employees?

---

13. Why is it equally important to secure the proper documentation when dealing with family and friends?

14. In what way is a general partnership dangerous for each of the partners?

Being Deceived by Your Partner

Why Trust Is So Important

What Due Diligence and Fiduciary Duty Are All About

Nathan Greengrass had been in business before; some of his businesses were successful, others not so successful. He was ready to try again. An opportunity came along for Nathan to become a partner in a small business that gave him a chance to return to an old love, writing. He put up some serious cash and proceeded to create a national magazine. It was an immediate success. It didn't guarantee a phenomenal profit in its first year, but its future was fairly well established.

Unfortunately, one of Nathan's partners, Patrick, with whom he created this venture and on whom he relied for the history of the company, failed to disclose that certain intellectual properties (IP) on which the core elements of the business were built, did not "actually" belong to Nathan's new company. They were essentially stolen from someone else. Since his partner had failed to explain this to Nathan before he invested substantial capital and started the magazine, Nathan was forced to do everything he could to settle the matter with the original owners of the IP. His partner, however, had so antagonized the real owners of the IP that settlement appeared out of the question. In fact, these original owners brought legal action against Nathan's company and against Nathan himself, notwithstanding his innocence in the matter.

Nathan had to defend the action in the hope of reaching a settlement at some point in time, as the action sought damages in the hundreds of thousands of dollars for "intentional misconduct." After a while, despite the success of the magazine, the legal costs of defending this action in the federal courts exceeded the profit of the magazine. During all of this time, Nathan had been sharing this experience with his spouse, who understood that the fault was not his but his partner's. His partner, of course, had no money of his own.

The real question became: Where does all of this end and how much will it cost? Although Nathan's spouse was not his actual legal partner in the business, she was certainly his actual legal partner in their finances. What should Nathan do under these circumstances? His spouse acknowledged the success of the magazine but also recognized the hole in the floor through which their savings were draining. The question of bankruptcy became a serious subject at the dinner table. Nathan and his spouse agreed that there was no reasonable alternative; the leaking of their savings had to stop. The business filed bankruptcy despite the success of the magazine.

- Do you think Nathan should have continued the fight in the hope of ultimate settlement?
- Do you think Nathan was negligent in not having examined the company more closely before he made his investment?
- Do you think Nathan was so enamored of the magazine venture that he was distracted from examining the company more closely?
- Do you think that Nathan placed too much trust in a person about whom he knew very little?
- Do you consider his spouse a real partner?

Misrepresentation

To "misrepresent" is essentially to give a meaning to something that is less than accurate. In a business context, decisions are made on information that is deemed to be accurate. Information presentations that are less than accurate, whether intentionally or unintentionally, will lead to decisions based on bad premises. Relying on bad information on a consistent basis will invariably lead to bad business decisions and problems in the operation of any business. The worst part of this problem is that bad information, used as a predicate, will continue to be bad even as good information is layered on top of it. In other words, the bad stuff will continue to infect even the best information subsequently obtained. You've got to get rid of the bad apple before the entire barrel becomes contaminated.

> A partnership is based primarily on trust and the proper attitude. Realizing the best results for the business is the highest priority, along with the willingness to adjust priorities.

Deception

The question of deception is somewhat more problematic. It can be a deliberate deception or something less intentional; however, it is a deception nonetheless. Decisions based on deceptive practices such as omitting material facts are certainly misrepresentations of sorts. The fractional difference between the two hardly deserves a distinction. Both, or either, are inimical to the best interests of every company in the business marketplace. Keep in mind that the obligation of every partner is to guarantee that the information being presented to other partners is the best information available, and that it has been examined to ensure both accuracy and credibility. Anything less than this level of diligence falls short of the basic obligation of every partner. This is known as fiduciary duty: the imperative that persons must deal with others as they would deal with themselves—that is, act in the best interest of another.

Determining which information is correct is the beginning of the problem. Much of the truth of things lies in the credibility of the source. Always consider the source of the information you receive. The source must be reliable if the information is to be reliable. The next question is whether the information is partial or complete. If there is any doubt that the information might be incomplete, any decision should be put off until you have what you would consider the complete picture. Anything less than a complete picture will often cause your decision to be completely out of line. If the deception or the misrepresentation is of a material nature, a contract between parties can be voided; litigation is often a child of this marriage of unethical conduct.

This is why the byword of the legal profession in all relationships is "due diligence." It is the responsibility of each person to ensure that he or she has done as exhaustive a search of the salient facts as possible. These are the facts on which he or she will predicate the most important business decisions.

Language in the Contract

Most people think that a good contract can eliminate misrepresentations and deceptions. It should be noted that this is not the purpose of most contracts. Contracts are designed to eliminate ambiguities and to ensure against bad memory. Contracts will rarely be effective in eliminating all misrepresentations and deceptions. Even the most carefully crafted language cannot replace the trust and candor that must exist in a successful business relationship. Most business advisors will explain that people with larceny in their hearts will rarely be put off by protective language in an agreement. If they want to swindle you, they will usually have a variety of alternative methods to make it happen. This is why due diligence, protective methods, and additional security are always better alternatives than depending on a good contract. This is not meant to prejudice members of the business community. It is merely a matter of caution to be exercised in normal business activities. And with respect to a partnership contract, you must understand that there is no language that can be designed to accommodate the myriad details involved in the day-to-day operation of a business. This is why trust must be the highest priority in every partnership.

The Critical Time Frame

Although most decisions can be made after appropriate consideration and contemplation, some situations require that a judgment be made on an immediate basis. The question of whether there is time to consider all aspects will often depend on the stakes involved. As a businessperson, this decision can be one of the more critical decisions you might be forced to make. The decision itself might even be secondary to the high priority of getting the business moving right away. Be careful that you understand the stakes here. Make sure that you are making your decision on the best

> A method for resolving disputes should be a high priority in preparing a partnership agreement.

possible information. Be sure that you are not predicating lives or futures on misinformation or information that has been cooked up and presented as a deception. In most cases, it is impossible to unring the bell.

Decisions Based on the Evidence

Trial lawyers will tell you that juries usually make their decisions based on "the best evidence" at a trial. The question is: What is the "best" evidence? There is forensic evidence, which has its impact from the sciences. There is real evidence, which is based on the existence of material items. There is witness testimony as evidence, the acceptability of which is based on the credibility of the person giving the testimony. But the jury's decision is based on an amalgam of all evidence. The more interesting question, perhaps, is the weight of the evidence and the percentage required to move the deciding body to a decision.

Preponderance of the Evidence

In civil actions, the requirement necessary to have a verdict on behalf of a person bringing a legal action is that there must be a "preponderance of the evidence." This usually means that the evidence suggests the facts are "more probable than not." Some people have utilized "the scale" in this context if the weight of the evidence drops one side of the scale.

Beyond a Reasonable Doubt

In criminal trials, the jury must find that the evidence points to a guilty verdict "beyond a reasonable doubt." Although the definition of reasonable doubt continues to have its detractors, the concept is not based on mere skepticism on the one hand and absolute certainty on the other. As one court noted, the evidence ought to be such as "would cause prudent men to hesitate before acting in matters of importance to themselves."

In the Business Context

When it comes to operating a business, what constitutes evidence that would cause prudent men to hesitate before acting in matters of importance? If it were your business, would you change the direction of your company on the basis of mere conjecture? Would you want to be relatively sure that your actions would not devastate the company and destroy all the successes that you've managed to build over the years? Even conventional wisdom would suggest that you examine the genesis of your information, that you look for the predicate on which information has been reported. Business at its worst is based on calculated risks, risks that have been carefully analyzed to ensure that the most accurate information is the basis for the decisions. It is certainly not based on gambling. Calculated risks may be behind many business decisions. Gambling belongs in Las Vegas, where the big score equates with the probability of losing. Entrepreneurs can afford the calculated risk but not the gamble.

What about the Bigger Picture?

Have the people you trusted made good decisions based on the best evidence? The bigger question ought to be, What should the judgment be based on when evidence is somewhat conjectural? On what basis should the evidence be accepted that would cause prudent men to hesitate before acting in matters of importance? The real answer is based on the equation of risk vs. danger. If the risk is great but the potential loss is minor, then thin and unconfirmed evidence might be enough to move a decision forward. On the other hand, if the risk is great and the results represent, for example, the loss of human life, you would think that "thin and unconfirmed" just might not be good enough. Do you wonder what decision you might make if this kind of problem were put to the test of your

> Make sure you understand the facts, the alternatives, and the implications before taking a stand on a business decision.

best judgment? Is it a good idea to wait for patent protection before you spend money in the business marketplace to launch your product? What if the investment dollars were small? Do you think Nathan jumped into the business too quickly? Do you think he should have pursued his due diligence before investing? Do you think his investment was large enough to warrant additional diligence?

With Respect to Partnerships

Relying on the trust of your partner will always be the most solid ground for decision making. Each partner must assume that the benefit to the business is the highest priority of every other partner. If not able to accept this dictum, the partnership will face its ultimate challenge.

Worksheet Questions

1. Does it make any difference if a misrepresentation is intentional or unintentional?

2. Why is due diligence so important in a negotiating session?

3. Do you think that careful language will always avert a problem in a contract?

4. Why is trust the highest priority in every partnership?

5. Do you think that "evidence that would cause prudent men to hesitate before acting in matters of importance to themselves" is a good protocol to follow?

CHAPTER
18

Parents as Partners

The Good, the Bad, and the Ugly

The Dangers of Family Involvement
The Word "Parents" Means any Family
Member or Close Friend

Al Fallwell was especially knowledgeable in the instant printing business and, after working with his parents for a number of years, took
over the entire operation. He operated the business very well for over
a decade during which his parents went into retirement. In fact, he
grew the business quite dramatically. Then he hit a downturn and the
business verged on the edge of disaster.

The landlord, the franchise company, and the equipment companies all came after Jane and Ardell Fallwell, his mother and father,
both of whom had signed the original franchise lease and loan agreements. At this point, both had been retired for a number of years and

neither was capable of operating the business since neither had been involved in the business for quite a while. They weren't even aware of the business's day-to-day activities, but all their assets were still vulnerable as a result of their original signatures.

This business has made all kinds of arrangements for readjusting its debts, and will probably survive. In this case of a permanent takeover, arrangements could and should have been made, closing out certain obligations after a given time period to let the folks off the hook, providing the business showed proper stability in the early stages of transition, which it did. In fact, this applies to any partner who exits a business.

Moving their business into the hands of the next generation is a dream held by many parents. The children recognize the great opportunity that such a transition provides. It is unfortunate that, in the face of this joy, there are pitfalls to which little or no serious consideration is given—until it is too late. If you are involved in such a situation, make sure that the transition focuses appropriate attention on the ongoing responsibilities of current management and the release of all ongoing obligations of those exiting the business. This is important in any exit strategy, whether with parents as partners, friends as partners, or strangers as partners. The same attention should be paid to noncompete protection applicable to the exiting partners.

Make sure that all investments, particularly in the early days, are discussed, analyzed, and agreed on, rather than allowing individual, inexperienced judgments to prevail. It is in the nature of youth to reach out creatively toward the future. It is in the nature of parents to reflect on the past to ensure a conservative approach to the future. Neither is wrong. It is, in fact, in the combination of these outlooks that you will find the most successful transitions. It is worthwhile to take the time for this exercise. Discuss all of this with your professional before consummating the transaction.

All In the Family

Very often, parents or other relatives become the early investors in the entrepreneur's business venture. The reason is obvious. These are the people who trust the integrity of the person and have had experience with his or her background, education, and character. There is nothing wrong with these dollars from any standpoint. The real problem is in the casual attitude that one or both parties take toward the relationship. The standard that ought to be followed is that the family's investment deserves the same dignity as the stranger's. In other words, be sure to put everything in writing to protect both parties so that there is no surprise in the expectations of either.

> Make sure the family gets the same formality of paperwork you would give to someone outside of the family. This includes a credible business plan as well as evidence of their equity position in the business.

The Basis of the Relationship

The positive aspect of investing in someone you know is that you've usually had experience with him or her on a personal level. The negative aspect is that you've likely enjoyed a more emotional relationship and have not really analyzed the person from the perspective of their business acumen or intellectual capabilities. The fact of the matter is that any business investment of this kind is usually made on the basis of good faith and not on the basis of knowledge and experience. It is more in the nature of helping out than of analyzing the business from the standpoint of potential profit. Some parents and family members have actually equated such an investment with furthering the education of a member of the family. If this is, in fact, the thinking of the investor, then make sure it remains as such. One of the problems is that this "furthering the education concept" often evolves into a business analysis, and the original gratuitous intent gets lost in the search for profit.

Investing Is One Thing

The budding entrepreneur's parent or friend must make a judgment as to the extent of the loss that they might incur and their ability to handle such a loss. This is just like the situation of a shareholder in a corporation, who is responsible only to the extent of his or her investment. The real danger is not in the cash investment. It is in the continuing obligation. If the entrepreneur does not have the appropriate borrowing ability, he or she is likely to ask the investor to cosign a note or act as a

> Be sure that the investment is not going to negatively affect their quality of life or their expectations for retirement.

> **D**on't ask them to cosign or guarantee a long-term obligation.

guarantor. In such a case, that signature could have long-term consequences, far beyond the loss of the original investment. Parents have often signed lease contracts or franchise agreements or even bank loans that extend liability far beyond the expectations of the average investor. If the business falls apart, we know that the creditor will always go after "the deepest pockets" even though the person signing the contract or the lease or the loan may have had little or nothing to do with the business. If the company should file bankruptcy, for example, the guarantor is liable for the entire balance of the obligation. This is a real danger and ought to be considered with the greatest caution!

A Contract Is Not for the Ill-Intentioned

Another problem inherent in dealing with family is that the handshake or the hug often seals the deal. The minimum protection that should be afforded to a member of the family is a contract of some kind, drawn at the time the money is made available.

> *A Legal Suggestion*: The money being delivered to Charline Brown is for investment in her company. Twenty percent of these dollars will be for the purchase of 2,000 shares of the business representing 10 percent of the ownership. These shares will be evidenced by stock certificates in my name with anti-dilution language attached. The balance of 80 percent of these dollars will be a loan to the company, represented by a promissory note to be paid in monthly increments of both principal and interest, bearing interest at 7 percent per annum, and with the payments beginning on January 1, 2008. There will be a penalty of 10 percent of the existing principal balance for late payments made later than ten days after due date, and a default clause for acceleration of the entire balance in the event any payment is not made within 20 days of the due date.

The above is not designed to be all-inclusive, but represents the thinking of the parties at the inception of the loan/investment. It should always be remembered that contracts are not for those whose intentions are suspect. Conventional wisdom should tell you that if you are dealing with people who have larceny in their hearts, they will probably "getcha" if that is their intention. Contracts are basically designed to eliminate ambiguities in language and to clarify false memory. By putting language in a document that references the intent of the parties, it is less likely that conflict will take place because of someone not understanding the nature of the relationship, or because each person has a different recollection of the arrangement. It is good protocol between and among strangers; it is mandatory to maintain good relations between and among family and friends.

> The combination of investment/loan is usually the most comfortable method of investment for parents, family, and close friends.

Working Together

The final aspect of the parents-as-partners scenario is when the partners are working together in the same business. Whether the younger or the elder generation started the business, the problems remain the same. Similarly, regardless of how much each may have invested in the business, the problems of decision making will always need to be addressed.

The Reverse of the Generation Gap

Parents are not always the creators of the business into which the son or daughter is integrated. In some cases, the business is actually started by the younger generation, with the elders brought in to fill the gaps and help them to maintain their dignity by contributing to the continuity of the business. It also allows them to earn a salary as well as a position in the family success. Here again, unfortunately, the responsibilities of the opportunity may be beyond the scope of their experience or education. Interestingly, the younger generation usually expects less of their parents than the parents, in other circumstances, would have expected from the children. The "children" recognize that innovation over the past few decades

> Treat them with the same dignity you would afford to an outside investor.

has brought the level of general business sophistication to a place far beyond the normal education or experience of their parents. Not always true, but usually the perception.

The Root of the Problem

When family is involved, the question of hierarchy becomes of paramount importance. The elders will often think that the younger generation is brash, untested, and too quick in making decisions without proper forethought. The younger generation, on the other hand, is often too quick to criticize the elders about their more conservative, practiced, and historically correct attitude toward change. The question as to who is responsible for the ultimate decisions needs to be clarified long before the need for decision making becomes critical to the business. As in a partnership, an understanding of obligations and prerogatives is key to the management team functioning properly.

Sibling to Sibling

Even more significant and problematic than parent and child is the relationship between siblings—between participants of relatively equal stature. Even in cases where one sibling has a more significant education than another, this does not necessarily support the case for more power or decision-making authority. It can be very much like a franchise, in which the franchisor likely knows more about the business at the beginning of a venture, but the franchisee invariably knows more about the customer base and the limited geography of the business activity after being in business for some time.

It is always in the best interest of the business to continually reappraise each business category and, on a periodic basis, the capability of the person in charge of each activity. Don't lock your thinking into a precedent of hierarchy without having a good reason to maintain it.

Worksheet Questions

The word "parents" refers to any family member or close friend.

1. If you expect your parents' involvement, have you presented them with a credible and professional business plan?

2. Do they understand that they might not get their money back?

3. Do they understand that reinvestment for growth will likely preclude any early distribution of profit?

4. Will they expect to participate in the business as a result of their investment?

5. Do they expect to have someone on "The Board" to monitor expenditures?

6. Would a loss of the entire investment affect their quality of life?

7. Would a loss of any portion of their investment affect their retirement plans?

8. Have you considered the previous question?

9. Is any portion of the investment designated as a loan to be paid back by the business?

10. Have you given them stock certificates or other indicia of their investment in the company?

Arbitration and Mediation

When Partners Don't Agree

The matter of business decisions became a serious problem for a garment manufacturer, whose private company was owned 50–50 by him and his wife. Of course, the underlying problem of a pending divorce didn't make the situation any easier. Since the husband, Alan Broadbent, was the precipitating cause, having left the business as well as the bedroom, there was an initial assumption that when the buyout exercise between the partners was finished, his wife, Geraldine, would be the owner of the business. Geraldine was in a position where building the business to the next level was the appropriate thing to do. In this same context, however, Alan's choice was to maintain the status quo so that the value of his buyout in cash would be greater. The lawyers representing each party in this divorce were unable to find an answer to this conundrum.

The Ombudsman

A year or so before this situation had become critical, Alan and Geraldine had decided to get the business valued for possible sale to a third party. (One or both might have anticipated that their ongoing relationship was not going to prevail over the long term.) The person they agreed to use for this valuation was Nathan, in whom both reposed a certain degree of trust. They even prevailed on him to join them on a consulting basis to help both move the business to the next plateau of success. Recognizing that the failure of Alan and Geraldine to agree on basic business decisions could be detrimental to the future of the business, Nathan agreed to help. Both attorneys felt that this would be best for the business, and would also alleviate part of the problem in the divorce proceeding. It was in this context that the attorneys recommended that the court confirm the designation of Nathan as the ombudsman and the mediator. The court put it this way: "In the event of a dispute concerning a major decision regarding the business, Nathan shall act as arbitrator and shall have the authority to make a binding decision." This language essentially made Nathan the chief operating officer of the company during this difficult period.

Time and Circumstances Change the Game

Although Nathan tried to be fair in his judgments about the company, the fact was that the company was at a crucial phase in its development. As a result, Nathan authorized the company to make certain expenditures in order to maintain its relationship with some substantial customers. For example, it needed to build a more sophisticated software system and this was an expensive proposition. It was this kind of decision making that caused Alan to feel less comfortable with Nathan's position at the company. However, since the court had already designated Nathan as the decision maker, Alan's position, in a sense, had deteriorated in terms of maintaining control.

Designated Arbitrator Notwithstanding

In its agreement designating Nathan as the mediator, the court also appointed him as one of the arbitrators in the event that it became necessary to resolve the ultimate question of ownership through the buyout process. Since Nathan had been working closely with Geraldine during this period when Alan was absent from the business, Alan felt uncomfortable with Nathan's participation and, through his attorneys, objected to Nathan's continuing role as an arbitrator.

Candor and Honesty

Although Nathan wasn't really interested in staying on in his arbitrator role, Geraldine's attorneys felt that he should at least write a letter to the court and have the court make the ultimate decision. Nathan felt that, notwithstanding his continuing role as consultant to the company, he would still be able to be objective as an arbitrator. However, he also felt that it was necessary to be honest with the court about his position.

The Letter

In his letter to the court, Nathan explained: "I have certainly spent more time with Geraldine than with Alan." He even went on to say, "I have, as a result, a better understanding of her goals than I do of his, as she has been more forthcoming with regard to conversations, questions, etc." And finally, he had to admit that "I am more likely to continue in my role as 'consultant to the company' on a transitional basis in the event that Geraldine becomes the owner than if Alan becomes the owner." Because of this candor, the court decided to dismiss Nathan as one of the arbitrators.

This story should tell the reader a great deal about the roles of a mediator and an arbitrator, and the context in which each serves.

The First Order of Business

All partnership contracts should have mediation or arbitration clauses; however, the shortest route to resolution without resorting to a more formal approach is to designate an ombudsman, a single person, in whom both repose a certain degree of trust and who can mediate between the parties to find a solution or, in lieu of that, who can make a decision to move the business forward. This has proven to be extremely

> All partnership agreements should have a mediation or arbitration clause.

helpful, especially to the small-business community. The ombudsman can be a lawyer, another professional, or merely a person who knows something about the business. It's an appropriate method of resolution at various stages of growth. With two people, an engineer and a sales professional, for example, the early days of a business venture may require more of the engineer's time and experience, during which period most of the decisions would likely be his or hers. In later stages, the salesperson's time and ability may be the higher priority, as decision-making prerogatives change. At any stage, however, the best decisions are those that will accelerate the growth of the business or resolve any problems before they become pending disasters.

As good, as honest, and as flexible as two partners might be, it is inevitable that there will be business decisions on which the two do not agree. Disagreements that create serious problems can dramatically affect the progress, or even the ultimate success, of the business. If there is a 50–50 equity representation, as opposed to a 51 percent majority, the partners must create a format that will allow the company to move forward notwithstanding a serious difference of opinion. In fact, even if there is a majority opinion, a format for dispute resolution will help to eliminate a decision that will cause disruption to the decision-making process. Don't let the molehill become the mountain. Remember the adage, "Into every life a little rain must fall." In business, you've got to be sure that you treat the "little rain" for what it is and not let it become a hurricane. It's much easier to solve the problem when it's small and doesn't yet affect every other aspect of the business. Think of the dam improvements that could have been made before Hurricane Katrina made landfall. If you fail to attend to this problem at its inception, it will invariably become bigger than life, with its negative dynamics increasingly hard to handle.

> Don't ever let a dispute become a disagreement that will disrupt the business.

The first approach is likely to be negotiation with the other party in the hope that any formal confrontation can be avoided. This is where each party can achieve some measure of what he or she considers to be his or her entitlement without giving up too much in order to achieve the negotiated peace. This is called adjusting your priorities. If this is not possible because the parties are locked into their positions, or because the animus between the parties has made negotiating difficult, or because the ombudsman approach is not acceptable, then alternatives must be examined. Mediation is a method by which a third party causes the partners to reconsider each other's opinions. This is very much like someone playing devil's advocate without the emotional involvement of being a partner. Arbitration is a method by which the partners authorize a third party to make a decision on their behalf after hearing all the salient facts. The alternative to these approaches may be to go to court. This is where each side will present the evidence, and the court, a judge, or a jury will make the decisions. The time, cost, and embarrassment of this procedure should make it the court of last resort. And don't ever lose sight of the fact that after the expenditure of money and emotional capital, the partnership will never again be able to function in accordance with good business protocol.

Conflict Resolution

Mediation and arbitration are less onerous, costly, and time-consuming than the courthouse. Mediation is a less formal step. Although the third party, which listens to the problem, does not have authority to force a settlement, he or she can bring the facts to light in an objective way and suggest to both parties what a final disposition of a court might be. It is important that this individual have some background in the judicial system so that the parties will accept their cautions about the costs, emotional and financial, relative to an actual trial. This "fear factor" is ordinarily sufficient to give the parties pause, inspiring them to adjust their expectations to find a middle ground to settlement. This will often have the effect of both parties becoming a little more conciliatory in their attitudes. It will often lead to at least a partial resolution of the more pressing matters, with other concerns being held in abeyance. Even though it might not be final, it is certainly informational and can be quite telling to the person who fails to prevail.

Background and Experience

Although there is no mandate to choose any particular person—and it is quite possible for the parties to agree to use a nonprofessional third party—common

> The highest priority of a mediator or arbitrator should be the success of the business.

sense would suggest that someone with the experience of having handled delicate matters in the past would likely be a better choice. There are mediators who have formal training and there are those who have experiential backgrounds. These are people who are used to dealing with the fundamentals of how to approach a problem. They have also dealt with personality conflicts. Most of them have experience in the business marketplace and usually know what can satisfy the participants. They have the experience to recognize that a particular middle ground is achievable.

Arbitration

Arbitration allows both parties to submit the controversy to an impartial third party, chosen by the parties to determine an equitable settlement. If the parties agree to be bound by this decision, the process is called "binding arbitration." This is one way to have the parties understand what an objective person might do in light of all the facts presented on both sides. It is much less problematic, less emotionally draining, less expensive, less time-consuming, and less cumbersome than the formality of a trial before a judge or jury. There are many organizations now that offer retired judges as both mediators and arbitrators. Either of these is certainly preferable to the long-term commitment of a court hearing. Speak to your professional before you make a decision that could have dire consequences for on the synergy of your partnership.

Legal Approach

In the event that the partners cannot reach a decision at any juncture during the course of business activity, it is agreed that a three-step approach will be utilized to avoid this stalemate.

To resolve the problem as quickly as possible, the partners might agree to appoint their friend, Jay Northrup, whom the partners trust to be objective in his judgment, to "hear" the matter from each partner's perspective and suggest the most advantageous approach for the best interests of the business.

In the event that the partners fail to conform to Jay's recommendations, the partners will agree on a different third party in whose hands they will place the responsibility of suggesting resolution to the problem.

In the event that the partners fail to agree to the recommendations of either Jay or another third party, the matter will be referred to a different third party for binding arbitration. The parties will agree on an arbitrator. Failing to agree on an arbitrator, each party will appoint an arbitrator, and the two arbitrators will agree on a third arbitrator. In this fashion, each party will be represented and the third appointee will be in a position to break any tie that may result in the resolution process.

> Be sure you understand all the available approaches to conflict resolution.

Worksheet Questions

1. How will the appointment of an ombudsman help the decision-making process?

2. Does the ombudsman have to be a professional such as a lawyer or an accountant?

3. Why is "adjusting priorities" the best answer to most partnership problems?

4. Why is litigation the worst of all possible approaches to a partnership dilemma?

5. What is the method used by a mediator?

6. What kind of experience and background should a mediator have?

7. What is the method by which an arbitrator addresses a partnership problem?

8. Why is it best to put something in your partnership agreement about conflict resolution?

CHAPTER 20

Managers as Owners

And Other Partnership Relationships

Treat Them Like Partners
Even if They're Not

Barbara had a very successful print shop in Utah. It had exceeded her expectations. Its success was predicated in great part on her ability to deal with customers in a very singular way. She would waive the charge for graphics if the order was substantial enough. She would delete all delivery charges for customers who were consistent in purchasing. She was a strong person who monitored her relationships very carefully and kept close watch on her cash flow to ensure that these tradeoffs didn't lead to customers taking advantage. As the saying goes, she ran a tight ship. She did not share these special deals with her employees because she was a hands-on entrepreneur who did most of the selling herself. She had already experienced a

181

salesperson quitting and taking his "loyal customers" with him to another printer. She wasn't going to let this happen again.

Unfortunately, Barbara's mother in Colorado got very ill. Because Barbara was an only child, her mother's illness required Barbara's presence for long periods of time; finally, she was needed for an extended period, during which time her mother was in hospice care.

These absences resulted in Barbara leaving the operational responsibilities to her manager, Marge. Marge was happy to take on the responsibilities but was not privy to the special deals, nor to the requirements of the line of credit with Barbara's bank, nor to the existence of some small, minority shareholders in the business to whom Barbara mailed a narrative report each week. While given the responsibility for management, Marge did not receive the necessary information or the authority to manage the business properly.

It didn't take long for a number of things to happen:

- One substantial customer got billed for graphics work and got upset. This led to a failure of the customer to pay the bill. Without the owner around to resurrect the relationship, this account was lost. Even collection of the bill became questionable.
- Because the bank had not been apprised of the weekly cash-flow position of the company, it sent a letter cancelling any additional funds in the line of credit.
- Another substantial customer got angry when she was told that delivery charges were going to be applied in the future. This was actually a positive, aggressive move on Marge's part to compensate for the loss of credit with the bank. That decision, in isolation, was one that Barbara agreed with.

The last problem that she faced was with one of the minority shareholders who had not received her weekly report from Barbara. This person berated Marge, who knew nothing of this obligation, and left her in tears.

Barbara's mother passed away and Barbara returned to Utah to resume charge of the business. She had been away for three months. After trying to rebuild her customer base unsuccessfully, and seeking professional advice, Barbara filed bankruptcy and returned to her home in Colorado. She had lost her business and went to work for a local printer.

- Even if Marge were a genius, could she have operated the business without Barbara being more forthcoming?

- Did Barbara's business fail because the problems were beyond her control?
- Should Barbara have made Marge a partner in the business?
- Do you think this would have changed Marge's attitude or the attitudes of the customers?
- Do you think this would have been a good idea?

The word "partnership" encompasses a world of relationships. You can isolate it by referring exclusively to the legal definition of a general partnership, or you can open it up to all relationships having to do with the prerogatives and obligations of just about every business involvement. In this chapter, you will see just how the "business of relationships" works. The salesperson, the banker, the investor, the employee, the vendor, the customer—each has an impact and, to some extent, some power over the owner of a business.

> You must always give the necessary authority to the people who are responsible for getting a job done.

The Manager as Owner: Perception vs. Reality

One of the biggest problems facing entrepreneurs is allocating responsibilities to employees without giving them sufficient authority to carry out their duties. This gets even more dramatic as the employee is given greater responsibilities, including the actual management of the business. Although it is certainly true that owners do not want to forego all control over the business's decision making, they must be aware that asking someone to take their place without giving them the ability to do so is a self-defeating proposition. The control that they give can certainly be limited, but it must be commensurate with the job that needs to be done. There are many ways that the owner can continue to monitor the business in his or her absence without handcuffing the manager's range of motion. (For a careful analysis of these protections, see Chapter 11 on cash flow.)

The Salesperson Relationship: The "Partner" You Didn't Count On

One of the most interesting aspects of the printing business is that the person at the front counter is often the least respected and lowest-paid person in the company. This is the person who was taught how to bid a job, how to satisfy the customer when there's a problem, and how to establish a relationship with the customer that will keep him or her coming back to the same shop. There are many print shops within any given geographic area, all offering their potential customer multiple choices. The "relationship partner" that you put at the front counter is probably one of the most important employees that you have. And the title of relationship partner is certainly apt; even the banks now call the banker you use your "relationship banker."

The Real Problem with Loyalty

Loyalty to the company is only one side of the double-edged sword of loyalty to and from the customer. It is interesting that in a variety of businesses, the customer deals with the salesperson and often doesn't know and has never even met the owner of the company. Keep in mind that the concept of selling is often predicated on the proposition that it doesn't make much difference what the product or service is. It is the confidence that the consumer has placed in the salesperson that makes the sale happen. Certainly, the product or service must live up to its representations, but the initial sale is based on the trust and credibility inspired by the salesperson. If the salesperson leaves the company to work for a competitor, is it any wonder that the customer will follow the person, rather than the product? Loyalty really matters!

> Remember that your customers have as much loyalty to your salespeople as they do to the product or service itself.

Understanding and Dealing with the Loyalty Challenge

The concept of employer-employee is never more significant than when it deals with the owner of a business and the person to whom the owner gives the responsibility of meeting with the customer. On the one hand, the salespeople understand that they represent the company, and that all representations made by them are standards that the company must fulfill. This is one of the reasons why many contracts use the terminology: "All representations relating to the product or service sold must be in writing and signed by an officer of the company. The company will not be held responsible for any representations made by employees unless in writing and endorsed by management." Notwithstanding this caveat, this warning, many salespeople will use language such as: "Don't worry about it. I give you my word." And in most cases, the salesperson actually does take on the responsibility of "making it right" when something goes awry. Thus the phenomenon of loyalty to the salesperson, not to the product. With this in mind, it is understandable that many customers will follow the salesperson, not the product. So what happens when the salesperson decides to offer his or her services to the proverbial "competitor across the street," and takes the customers along to the new company? The answer is not a happy one. As discussed in the next chapter, although the partner in a business might be prevented from competing this way, the courts are very reluctant to hold employees to the same standard. This, then, fortifies the injunction to treat your employees with every bit as much respect as you would your partners.

How Then, Can I Deal with This?

Many business owners are quick to consider the legal approach to problems of this kind. Although examining the legalities is always a good idea in anticipation of a problem, some situations call for a more personal approach: 401Ks, profit sharing, recognition and respect, family time, holidays, special bonuses, cars, health insurance, and the like. And you can always make an employee a partner. There are many kinds of partnerships and many aspects to profits and control. A minority partner (shareholder) in a corporation or a "member" of an LLC may have an interest in the business but rarely has any prerogatives. Especially in a new business, the chance of a "distribution" to shareholders is unlikely. The usual scenario is for any profit to be reinvested in the business to spur its growth. When it achieves a certain plateau of success, the shareholders may then enjoy a distribution, but usually not before. As a result of this standard growth pattern, valuable employees are often vested with small percentages of ownership or, at least, profit. It creates a better stabilization of the business by locking the talent in place. In addition, it precludes the possibility, in many ways, of a competent employee examining the potential of becoming a competitor and taking customers away from the business.

The Problem with Vendors

> You must treat your vendors with the same kind of respect during your good days as you would like to be treated by them during your rough patches.

"Don't screw me when times are tough . . . They can get much tougher." Although you would not normally characterize a vendor as a partner per se, you ought not to lose sight of the concept of relationship partner. It is the interdependence that makes this arrangement valuable and makes each of the parties vulnerable. If you expect to get special treatment from your vendors in tough times, it is advisable to treat them consistently when your business is thriving. Don't forget about one hand washing the other.

One Hand Washes the Other

There was a time in the "quick-printing industry" when paper actually flooded the market. This was a time when some quick printers put the pressure on the paper companies they were dealing with to lower the price or lose the business. In subsequent years, the entire quick-printing industry suffered a variety of problems, not the least of which was saturation of quick printers in practically every marketplace. In addition, the proliferation of very sophisticated equipment and the introduction of computer software made every customer, to some extent, a quick printer of his or her own. Competition grew, margins got slimmer, and the worst part was that paper was in short supply. Quick printers tried to get favors from the paper companies, such as a longer period to pay the bill. The concept of one hand washing the other became the order of the day. For those quick printers who showed respect in the good old days, favors were available. For those who took advantage during those days, favors were not so easy to find. It's a simple lesson, but a good one.

The Problem with the Family

In some cases, the partnership is actually formed by integrating members of the family. In these cases, it's simply good business to treat the partners with the same dignity you would give to a stranger. In situations when the immediate family is not so bound on a legal basis, you should be careful to recognize their involvement nonetheless. Whatever they may forego in quality time, holiday and vacation time, and money for those "simple extras," the obligation deserves to be recognized. Many times they will show more good faith in you and your dreams than the person who actually invests cash in the company.

The Problem with Bankers

"You're not my partner so why do I need to supply you with all this information?" In many instances, you will choose to borrow from a lender in lieu of allowing an investor to own part of your company. But don't think that this alternative eliminates the need for you to share your expectations, your ideas, and your financial paperwork with the bank. Although you've avoided a technical partnership involvement, you are still obliged to inform the bank of the status of your company in all its aspects. You need to present a business plan to the bank that establishes the guidelines of your relationship at the outset. You should update this presentation consistently, in good times and in bad. They will be much more willing to help on a bad day if they feel you've treated them properly on the good days.

The Problem with Investors

"Don't tell me that the short road is better than the long road, just because you want to get your money back sooner."

You must remember that most investors don't really share your dream. They have a dream of their own. Their dream is a multiple return on their original investment in the shortest possible time. Your dream is to fulfill your greatest expectations, however long it may take. This is why the dichotomy of time between investors and entrepreneurs always exists. Although you wouldn't prostitute the goal by acceding to their primary interest, you must extend to them the appropriate respect in your decision making.

The Problem with Customers

"When the customer takes the bait and the price goes up because of demand, be careful. Remember, the relationship is a partnership of trust."

In every community, however large or small, a business will survive and prosper if it is a reliable and consistent "partner with the customer." When a business fails to maintain this high level of trust, the customer base will dwindle and the business will falter. It is interesting that in some communities, the customer may actually confront the problem and a resolution may be possible. In most communities, however, the customer is not as inclined to become so involved. They will merely eliminate that stop on their regular consumer rounds. And the owner of the business may never know why. Bad business methodology will, of course, add to the problem, bringing failure and even the demise of the business. And it is that simple. This is why good business protocol must be established. It should include, at the very least, the basic values of image, service, and quality. And don't ever forget that you can't do it alone. All your employees must be in sync.

The Problem with Employees

"Do unto others as you would have others do unto you . . . or I'm gone."

Today's relationship with employees cannot be a casual one. The days are gone when an employee will stay with the same company for a lifetime regardless of the changes in benefits, job obligations, etc. Depending on individual perspectives, you can attribute this to a variety of variables. The lure of entrepreneurship has led many individuals to establish their own businesses rather than accept the vulnerability of a job that may not be "a forever position." The success of franchising has certainly contributed to this phenomenon. It tells people that they can learn what they need to know to properly operate a business by following an existing, successful formula. Another reason for the change is simple greed. Our entire commercial society appears to be drowning in the dream of profit. One way to achieve this profit is to cut down costs, "expenses against revenues." By

> You must protect the continuity of your business by treating your employees with the appropriate respect.

outsourcing jobs to less expensive communities—often outside of the country—local people may lose their jobs, but the profit to the owner goes up. With the steady rise in health insurance premiums, companies tend to cut this benefit to save money—sometimes even to survive. All of this leads to that vulnerability, which theoretically is eliminated if you own your own business. This concept weaves throughout this book. It needs to be examined and reexamined by every potential partnership.

Worksheet Questions

1. Why should the word "partnership" be considered in a broader sense than just the legal?

2. Do you think that authority to carry out a job should be commensurate with the responsibility for getting that job done?

3. Should you continue to monitor your manager after giving him or her the reins of your business?

4. Do you know how to monitor your manager without limiting his or her ability to manage?

5. Why are some people called relationship partners?

6. Why should you revisit the question of how these people are treated?

7. Do you think your customers are more loyal to your product or to your salesperson?

8. What kinds of incentives can you offer to keep your employees loyal to the company?

CHAPTER 21

Diamonds Are Forever; Partnerships Are Not

The Disparity Among Partners

Bill was a lawyer who decided to enter into a partnership with three other lawyers. The problem with forming this partnership was that each of the partners came into the business at different levels of financial participation. One lawyer, who had been in business as a sole practitioner for some time, actually brought in a client base that represented about 45 percent of the total income of the new partnership. A second partner brought in about 25 percent of the partnership's income, but his practice was exclusively devoted to divorce work, which other members of the firm did not handle. A younger partner with no practice of his own signed a promissory note, agreeing to buy into the partnership over a period of years. His partnership interest, based on the value of the partnership when he joined, would be 15 percent. The last of the partners was Bill, who came from another law firm with a small but active practice. He was allocated 15 percent of the partnership based on the practice he was bringing in. They agreed to take equal salaries and split the profits according to their percentages: 45:25:15:15. At the end of each year, the group would make a judgment as to how much new business each had brought to the firm, and the percentages would be adjusted accordingly for the following year. The amount of work handled by each partner, based on hours, would then adjust the salary base, as any partner might be called upon to handle new clients, whether he brought them in or someone else did.

Bill, who was the most sales-oriented of the partners, generated more new business than all the other partners combined. But his other partners were handling many of Bill's new clients because he was devoting most of his time to getting new clients. The youngest partner was still finding his way into the business community. The oldest partner, with 45 percent of the business, was already thinking about retirement and was more interested in spending time with his family than in building a bigger business base. The partner with the divorce practice just kept rolling along with his own practice. Bill was angry that he was spending so much of his time building the business. Although he would benefit to some degree from his new business, so would everybody else. Bill didn't think it was fair.

❑ ❑ ❑

- Do you think Bill's position is reasonable? Do you think he might have anticipated much of this before he entered the partnership?
- Do you think Bill might have thought differently if he had been given more money for the clients that he brought into the firm, even though they may have been handled by one of his partners?
- Do you think that this is the best way to handle such a partnership?
- Do you think that Bill should consider leaving the partnership?

At the beginning of any business partnership, the partners usually envision a long-term relationship; otherwise, they would not be so willing to invest their time to share anticipated benefits with someone else. Unfortunately, expectations notwithstanding, longevity is often limited. As previously discussed, the goals and expectations of the individual partners will change at least to some degree over a period of time. This is why an exit strategy must be developed by and between all partners. It will ensure that if one partner leaves the company, his or her absence will not destroy the integrity of the company and its ability to stay afloat.

Many Reasons to Revisit the Original Partnership Concept

There are many ways to redesign a partnership and there are many reasons to do so. Although many times the reason is that the partners have a substantial disagreement about a material aspect of the business, this is not always the case. Over time, the goals and expectations of people are bound to change. Raising a family mandates an entirely different approach to business than when one is single. Time must be divided to achieve success in both your personal and your business life. This is not easy to do and, in many cases, the family's principal earner is forced to limit time at the business in order to succeed at home. If the reverse happens—time is curtailed at home in order to succeed in business—the result can be devastating to the family. Don't think that this is an easy decision. Thousands of real-life stories speak to the contrary. When this dichotomy becomes the principal problem, the partnership becomes both the problem and the solution. In some cases, arrangements can be made for substituting people, or reducing salaries. In other cases, the problem is not resolvable and the partnership needs to consider more drastic steps.

Anticipating the Problem

The purpose of this book is to examine various business aspects in the context of a working partnership. It involves essentially all relationships that the entrepreneur needs to negotiate to succeed in business and maintain that success. Note the many examples in the previous chapter. The main idea is to anticipate what problems may arise in any of these relationships and to be prepared before the problem arises. The biggest challenges are the ones that are closest to home . . . problems within the working partnership itself. The

> It is mandatory, early on, that you develop a method for a partner to exit a partnership without destroying the integrity of the business.

partnership agreement is based on each partner having the responsibility for job performance, whatever it may entail. When one partner is absent, those responsibilities fall on the shoulders of the remaining partner or partners. When one partner dies, the resulting problems can be devastating to the business. This is why partnerships should carry key man insurance. The purpose of this insurance is to ensure the continuity of the business and to prevent the remaining partners from inheriting a spouse or other beneficiary of the deceased partner through a will or intestate succession.

The Buyout

In the event that a partner wants to leave the partnership, there are a number of approaches that can be used. One of these is for the exiting partner to have his or her equity position acquired by the other partner or partners. The one aspect of this buyout that should be sacrosanct is the continuity of the business. Very much like protecting a child of divorce, the business must be the highest priority. Although there are many more subtle considerations in the exiting of a partner, the payout of money is usually the prime element. If the company is making money, the buyout of a minor percentage of equity is no problem. If, on the other hand, the company is still in its growth period and money is tight, careful consideration must be given to the method by which the payout is scheduled. In some cases, the company itself will buy the equity position of the exiting partner and retire the shares. This will increase the value of the existing shares and all remaining partners will find that their equity positions are greater as a result. In some cases, one or more of the partners may buy the exiting partner's interest, in which case only their individual equity positions will be enhanced. In small enterprises, where there are only two partners, for example, the problem may be that neither the company nor the remaining partner is in a position to make the buyout. Do you think this problem is different when dealing with a partnership of professionals, such as doctors, accountants, or lawyers?

Right of First Refusal

Although key man insurance may prevent the remaining partners from "inheriting" a new partner at the death of a partner, a "living, exiting partner" usually has the right to sell his or her shares in the business to a third party not already in the partnership mix. This right, however, is usually coupled with some protection for the remaining partners. In a typical partnership arrangement, all partners are given a "right of first refusal" in the event that any partner chooses to sell his or her interest to a third party. This means that if the exiting partner chooses to sell his or her shares to a third party, each of the remaining partners has the opportunity to accept this offer, thus preventing a stranger from joining the partnership. Note, however, that the acceptance must be *exactly* the same as the original offer. If it is different in any substantial way, the right of first refusal doesn't apply. If a remaining partner fails to exercise this right within the appropriate time frame, then the third party may buy the interest. In a larger partnership, where this equity position constitutes a minor percentage of the company, it is less important. In a smaller partnership, where the equity position might be half of the equity in the company or a large enough percentage, coupled with others, to control the company, these elements are particularly important.

> Make sure that the right of first refusal is included in the agreement.

The Question of Money

It is unusual for any exiting partner to get a return of his or her investment completely at the time of the exit. This should always be addressed at the beginning of the partnership to avoid the possibility of disturbing or destroying the integrity of the company. This can happen when the payout dollars deplete the cash reservoir of the company, impairing its ability to function. In some cases, in fact, the result of not preparing for such a situation early on can cause the business to be sold in the event of a partnership breakup. Although the remaining partner or partners may be able to remain with the company as part of the transaction, this was not likely envisioned by any partner at the outset of the original partnership relationship. Do you think this is different in a professional partnership? What would you think if you were a client of one of these professionals?

Is There a Way to Do This?

Keep in mind that an exiting partner might not be leaving because the business is unsuccessful. There are many reasons for a partner to leave that may have nothing to do with the success or lack of success of the business. If the business is in financial trouble, all of the above scenarios may be applicable. If the business is successful and/or is showing great potential for the future, there are other ways for a remaining partner to handle the situation. If the partners had foresight at the beginning of the partnership, they probably agreed to have the business valued at various stages of its growth, normally once a year. By doing this, the value of the business is never in contest and the amount of any payout is determined objectively. The agreement would then go on to discuss the ability of the business to pay certain sums at certain times. With an appropriate down payment and the balance of the payout drawn over a designated period of time, the problems of payout and protecting the integrity of the company become much less problematic.

> Make sure you have an arbitration or mediation clause in the agreement.

A Legal Approach

In order to prepare for the possibility of partnership dissolution or the exiting of one or more partners, the partners, by being signatories to this agreement, agree as follows:

1. They shall have prepared each year, within 90 days of the close of the year, a valuation done by a person or firm designated by the parties. Should the parties fail to agree on a specific person or firm, then each partner will submit the name of a person or firm and these persons or firms shall agree on a third person or firm. If two of the three persons or firms designate a valuation within 10 percent of the other, then the average of these two valuations shall be accepted by the parties. If there is no

such percentage available, then the average of the three valuations shall prevail as the value of the business at that time.

2. The parties shall use these same people or firms to determine the amount of the payout, both down payment and incremental payments for the balance of the payout, that will allow the business to maintain its continuity in the face of these payments. They will consider, among other things, the cash reservoir necessary to maintain purchase of inventory or component parts necessary to produce inventory, the personnel necessary to maintain at least the current sales position, maintenance of all equipment necessary for adequate production, and all other elements necessary and appropriate to maintaining the business.

3. The parties shall also prevail on these same people or firms to suggest methods by which the payout might be adjusted, upward or downward, based on the success of the business and its ability to pay either more or less during the incremental payback of the balance of the payout.

The above represents one approach to the question of "paying out the agreed value of the percentage being purchased" and "allowing the company to survive during this critical period." The absence of a partner, for example, might entail hiring another person to take his or her place on the business team. Contingencies of this nature must also be "plugged in" for the protection of the company. There are many other ways to create these protections. Be sure to see your professional before deciding on the language to be used.

> You should arrange for a business valuation to be performed at least once a year.

Another Approach to Take

In the event that the remaining partner or partners don't have the available capital to accommodate the exit strategy, or the parties choose not to sell the business, there are yet other ways to approach the problem. Using the valuation of the business as a predicate, the remaining partners might consider the possibility of restructuring the business by inviting a new participant into the business as an investor.

Another Legal Approach

In order to interest an investor, the package will usually include the following:

1. A business plan explaining the growth potential of the business and the exit strategy contemplated for any investor.
2. A combination of debt and equity (part loan and part investment) in the business. This means that part of the dollars will be repaid with interest over a given period of time, and the balance will buy an equity interest in the business, allowing that portion of the investment, optimistically, to energize the business and return a multiple of that investment over a given period of time.
3. It will be agreed that a certain portion of this package will be used to buy out the exiting partner and another portion of this package will be used to enhance the growth potential of the business.
4. The money will be used by management without the advice and consent of the investor providing only that the company achieves certain plateaus of success within certain time frames. To monitor this success, the investor shall be entitled to serve on the company's board of directors.

Again, there are many ways to design this kind of restructuring. You must consider that most private-equity firms that might be interested in such an opportunity are also interested in the exit strategy. Their attitude is that they expect a return of 20 times their investment within a three- to seven-year period. Their expectations will usually be recognized by virtue of a sale of the business. This is one of the reasons why such a strategy is more of a stopgap solution. For those entrepreneurs who want to retain their business over the long term, be careful. *Be sure to speak with your professionals before embracing this kind of solution.*

Protecting Against Dissolution

Keep in mind that a formal legal partnership can be automatically dissolved with the exit of one partner. For this reason, partners will invariably convert their partnership to a written agreement to a corporate entity or an LLC early on. The corporation or the LLC will maintain its continuity in the face of any exiting partner or partners.

Although this chapter speaks to the issue of partnership dissolution, do not lose sight of the positive features of partnership. Partnerships are the relationships of people-to-people and people-to-business. Just like competition, partnership is a force that deserves respect as one of the main drivers of the business marketplace.

What Makes a Partnership Fair?

When you take your company into a joint venture with another company, each business makes an initial assessment of the value of the synergy involved. It is rare that both parties bring an equal value to the table. It is even more rare to have that value remain equal after the initial phase of the relationship. Why should a partnership between two people be any different? If it isn't different, then how do the parties work out a program that makes each feel comfortable in the short term as well as in the long term relative to partnership responsibilities?

Diversity of Expectations

In many cases, the entrepreneur needs a partner with money and an investor needs a partner with creativity or experience. The problem often stems from the fact that both parties consider themselves creative. It is the objective understanding of the reality that allows two or more people to establish a teamwork environment that will help a business to prosper. In many cases, one partner has a diversity of interests and the other partner is totally obsessed by the business at hand. In other cases, one partner may want a more laid-back quality of life with family, friends, and the tennis court. The other partner may feel, and not inappropriately so, that the investment of time must be dynamic on the part of all parties until the business reaches the stage where free time may be enjoyed. One of the problems in business is that some partners never feel that the business has reached this plateau.

Return of the Dollar

Although it is normal for an investor to take "stock for money," with his or her return based exclusively on the success of the company, this is not the only way to address a partnership where one of the people involved delivers the bulk of the working capital. Even though one partner may have the expertise, the one with the money may deserve to see a return of the investment *before* there is an equal distribution of salary or dividend. In a lot of ways, this approach eliminates a good deal of the pressure between partners. It is appropriate to remember that, creativity notwithstanding, the business would never have left the ground were it not for the investment capital involved in the early stages of development. This is good enough reason for the investing partner to see a return OF his or her investment before both partners can begin to enjoy the return ON the investment.

> Make sure you understand return OF investment and return ON investment.

Divorce in a Partnership

There is a business axiom that says: "Diamonds are forever; partnerships are not." Although not necessarily inevitable, it is understandable that most partnerships will be limited in time. As a result, it is always a good idea, while the parties are in good spirits, to make arrangements appropriate to each of the parties as well as to the business itself. It is not unusual for one partner or another to feel that he or she is contributing more, or participating more, and deserves more of the partnership profit. For this and other good reasons, there should be an opportunity for each to buy out the other based on a valuation formula agreed to at the beginning of the relationship. The written exit strategy is not unlike a prenuptial agreement.

The Ultimate Revisiting

At this time, there is a revisiting of the arrangement that created the original partnership arrangement—sometimes by both parties, but usually by one. It's great to have a format that will allow this problem to be resolved in a simple way. Unfortunately, time has a way of changing attitudes. And sometimes, animosity flares if the parties fail to communicate properly when the problem begins to show itself. Therefore, there should always be a mediation or arbitration clause that will allow a third party to intervene to the extent that some objectivity can be brought to bear in a situation that might otherwise be unsolvable. As you get involved in the positive aspect of examining the phenomenal potential for the growth of the business, be sure to include those provisions that will prevent the business from falling victim to two personalities that can't resolve their disputes. See your professional before this becomes a problem. Without the appropriate safeguards, the business itself will bear the brunt of the problem. This is not what anyone expects at the beginning of the relationship, nor is it what either party deserves as the relationship comes to an end.

Worksheet Questions

1. Why should an exit strategy be planned at the beginning of a partnership?

2. What is the problem of a partner dying without the company having key man insurance?

3. What should the highest priority be in the breaking up of a partnership?

4. Should the partnership agreement include a right of first refusal for the remaining partners?

---

5. Will creating a corporation or LLC prevent the partnership from automatically dissolving when the other partner exits?

6. Do you know the difference between "a return OF investment" and "a return ON investment"?

7. Do you think that an arbitration or mediation clause is necessary in a partnership agreement?

CHAPTER 22

Building a Decision Protocol

Knowing When to Hold 'Em and When to Fold 'Em

Some decisions are a lot harder than others. Patrick Elwin and Alvin Cordova were partners in a print shop that was just about holding its own. They lived and worked in a small southern town with a strong religious element. In fact, this religious element and the businesses associated with it represented the strongest part of their customer base. It was no surprise that they also owned and operated a religious bookstore. The bookstore was always losing money but was subsidized by the print shop. Both families were having a hard time living on their respective incomes, and the print shop was having difficulties maintaining its profit position.

Getting Advice that Hurts

The partners called on an old friend, who was also a business consultant, for advice. When the financial paperwork had been thoroughly and carefully examined, it was very clear that continuing to operate both stores was going to cause both to be closed and, quite probably, bring both partners to bankruptcy. The solution was disconcerting but clear. Either the partners needed to take less from the print shop, or the bookstore had to be closed. Patrick had very close ties to the community and felt that closing the bookstore would be seriously detrimental to his relationship with the community as well as his own personal self-worth. Alvin, who was quite a bit more secular and less religious, felt that to take a lesser income from the printing business would be detrimental to his family and to his obligations regarding his children's schooling and the like. He recognized the validity of the advice and took the position that survival dictated an uncomfortable but necessary course of action. The partners needed to agree on the solution.

Partners Getting to the Judgment that Counts

One of the reasons to have a partner whom you can trust is that another person's perspective can lend clarity to a situation that can easily get clouded in the personal struggle to succeed and prosper. Alvin knew that this judgment was difficult for Patrick to accept. He also knew, however, that the wrong judgment could be the end of the business and the partnership relationship that both partners held dear. He explained to Patrick that the community would understand the need for closure of the bookstore. He also assured his partner that when the printing business regained its strength and its profitability, he would certainly agree to reopen a religious bookstore. He was very sensitive to his partner's personal conundrum. It was this sensitivity that allowed Patrick to absorb the advice of his consultant and accept the inevitability of the situation. The bookstore was actually closed the following day—interestingly, on a Sunday. Both partners continued to operate the printing business. And they continued to respect the feelings of the other. This is what partnership is all about!

Conventional wisdom tells us that it's much easier to work with a partner in good times than it is in bad times. This is not necessarily so. There are some people, interestingly, who thrive on their ability to make good judgments in the face of threatening disaster. Others, of course, have a much easier time when the road is smooth. Be mindful of the fact that it's easier with cash in the bank than when borrowing to stave off disaster. You must be able to handle your business decisions in the face of either situation. And always, always seek professional advice when you see the storm clouds—not after the hurricane has wreaked its fury on your business and your future.

Business analysts point out that the failure of many businesses is not due to their inability to envision the next plateau of success; rather, it is their failure to anticipate the need for certain tools once they get there.

The Time Frame Differential

It is inevitable that the purchase of raw materials and components, as well as the building of a sales staff, will precede actual sales . . . and collections. This means that you will need substantial sums to produce the goods long before you receive the dollars from sales. This time-frame differential can be anywhere from days to months. Failure to recognize this gap has caused the demise of many otherwise successful companies. It's one thing to achieve that magic increase in sales; it's quite another to be in a position to handle it. Selling beyond your capability to produce can be disastrous. The alternative to this situation is the purchase of substantial equipment in anticipation of the expected increase in sales. The new equipment may give you the ability to produce, but it may take some time for customer recognition of your increased capability. It will take time for the money from the new sales to be commensurate with the cost of the equipment. It may be many months before the dollars from sales catch up with the immediate costs of the equipment. You need to determine if you have the capability of maintaining the company during this interim period.

> You must understand "the time-frame differential" when planning for the future.

The Negative of Accelerated Growth

Recognizing the problematic challenge of accelerated sales, the sophisticated manager may conclude that it might not be the best program to adopt. Is it better to have enough product for every customer at the expense of having excess inventory at the end of the season or to have too little inventory to fill every order but maximize the profit position of the company? Will the customer come back the following year? Each company has to answer these questions in its own way. It will be based on many short- and long-term goals.

The Hidden Part of the Equation

It is the hope, if not the dream, of every entrepreneur to move from the plateau of survival to the plateau of success. This kind of success is measured in dollars; the more successful entrepreneurs go on more trips, drive newer cars, and can afford to send their children to better schools. The creative, energetic, and knowledgeable businessperson has a better chance to achieve these goals than those people with fewer of these traits. The hidden part of the equation has to do with developments over which you have less control. These

> You must avoid the "putting out fires" concept as a tenet of management's long-term philosophy.

variables, of which there are many, are the challenges that make the difference. You've got to be prepared as best you can in the face of those exigencies. And the only thing you can do to prepare for those challenges is to think about tomorrow. A good business plan will help you anticipate the possibilities and prepare responses to them in advance. Stay ahead of the challenge and your game plan will be a success.

A Good Time to Think

Daily business activity for most entrepreneurs is all-consuming. Most decisions are made relatively quickly as problems arise. Thinking ahead, or creating proactive protocols, is not within the scope of normal business procedure. Yet this is exactly what stops most businesses from growing, getting to that next plateau of success, and contemplating negative possibilities early enough to avoid them. The common practice of "putting out fires"—handling problems as they occur—is to be avoided in the long-term planning of your business.

Maintaining the status quo may be a good idea when everything is clicking together and functioning well. It is, however, a "given" in business that such a situation is temporary at best. Waiting until the program stalls means you've waited too long. A good time to think about problems is in advance of having any. Being complacent in good times is the worst habit you can develop. Use this time to reflect on how you can improve your programs, anticipate the kinds of problems that could occur, and examine the alternative directions that your company can take in the event of unexpected change.

> You must understand that business decisions are your responsibility, regardless of the advice you get regarding business problems.

A Good Idea to Rethink Before It's Too Late

Many times in business you think, "If I do this, it will take away the problem for the moment," but you also know it's a "quick fix" that probably won't stand the test of time. You realize that an action has been put in motion that in some cases will take on a life of its own. This is why the experienced person will look carefully at the long-term implications before making short-term decisions. The time to contemplate ramifications is not after they happen with no opportunity to revisit the question. The time to reflect on that potential is before the fact. As you think of your business and the world that surrounds it, do your serious contemplating before you act.

Businesspeople

When it comes to seeking advice, businesspeople are of many minds, most of them in the camp of "those too embarrassed to ask." It is strange that even the most successful entrepreneurs don't quite understand that they can't be all things to all people. Some are embarrassed that they don't know as much as their accountant or lawyer; others are reluctant to admit that they failed to keep up with many of the nuances of their own business. The latter are more embarrassed than any others and usually refuse to recognize, let alone admit, that they are something less than expert in their field. It is a sad commentary on the small-business community. Entrepreneurs would do well to recognize their shortcomings. After all, we don't stop learning when we leave school, and we never know *all* there is to know about anything. The learning process is an ever-expanding circle, with things happening so quickly in just about every area that just keeping up is an unending program.

Worksheet Questions

1. Do you think that you and your partner can handle the business in bad times as well as in good times?

2. Do you believe that a proper business plan can alleviate this problem?

3. Do you think that "putting out fires" is good management protocol for normal business?

4. Do you think that a "quick fix" will handle the long-term problems of the business?

5. Are you "too embarrassed to ask" when you're looking for a solution to a problem?

6. Why is it necessary to be cautious when getting advice from an outsider?

CHAPTER 23

Growing in the Wrong Direction

Failing in Due Diligence

Tony Campbell was a very creative entrepreneur who, together with a small group of partners, opened a nightclub of sorts in Cambridge, Massachusetts. In a very short period of time the operation became a substantial success. Whether the success was due to the location, the proximity to Harvard University, the somewhat eclectic customer base (that was generated in great part by Tony himself), or other factors was never learned. The fact is that all elements appeared to be working toward this success. As time went on and this success seemed to hold, Tony and his partners were convinced that they had found the "secret" to success on the small-nightclub circuit. Even some of his competitors showed up on the notoriously slow Monday night to see what all the fuss was about. The crowd was still there.

209

The group of partners met one Sunday and decided that, with all this success, they ought to expand by opening in another location. Although there were some misgivings voiced by one very conservative partner, the rest of the group agreed. They opened their second location, in Hyannis, Massachusetts. The new operation was a total disaster! What happened?

Although not necessarily a problem in the establishment of new venues, (Starbucks® and Subway® being perfect examples of operations that have succeeded), geography is very important in some other types of business. The nightclub circuit is peculiar unto itself in that each area seems to have a core element that establishes the predicate for success. The sawdust on the floor, the subdued candle lighting, and the peanut shells all over the floor seemed to be attractors of success in Cambridge. They failed to capture the imagination of the locals in Hyannis. The location closed as quickly as arrangements could be made for a negotiated payout on the lease. Should the dissenting partner have been given more time and consideration in this matter? It is certainly something that warrants some examination. As a partner, make sure your opinion is heard, even when it appears to be the proverbial voice crying in the wilderness.

The Abnormal Fear of Competition

Speaking of geography as a problem in establishing multiple locations brings to mind a franchise in Britain. In England, the business marketplace is usually clearly defined and is normally found on "the High Street" of any given town. The franchise sales director, in an attempt to avoid the competition on High Street, purposefully crossed the river in a southern city to the residential side. When asked by the new managing director why he did this, his honest answer was "to avoid the competition on High Street." The problem was that all the businesses were on that same side of the river, not on the residential side. His job was taken over and the standard protocol set for new locations was that they be located only on the High Street and within 100 yards of a competitor's shop. Competition can actually be as helpful in some instances as it can be deleterious! The new shops quickly found their place in the sun: they made new customers of those who normally shopped on High Street, and certainly attracted some of their customers from the competition. Why do you think that McDonald's®, Burger King®, Taco Bell®, and others are usually within walking distance of one another? Be sure that you know just what "competition" is all about!

Make sure you understand the positive as well as the negative dynamics of competition, and where you fit into that spectrum in the marketplace.

Ideas Are Cheap

As previously discussed, if you want a lot of fresh, new ideas, all you have to do is go into a pub and buy a round of drinks. You will, invariably, end the evening with a bunch of ideas. The problem is that these ideas will evaporate when the pub closes. It is not the brilliance of the creator that builds a business. It is the constant attention to detail, the development of the appropriate protocols to establish method and direction, the discipline to implement those protocols, the dedication of people in the right places, the working capital to buy the necessary components, and the willingness to make changes when changes are indicated. Yes, those are a lot of things to think about when building a business, but make no mistake about it, a successful business does not happen by accident. Note the great idea in the Hyannis story—destined for failure for lack of due diligence in the implementation.

Money, the Necessary Component

An interesting problem to cope with is to have too much money at the start of a business. This may sound strange, but keep in mind that a business must be built in increments. You can't put the walls up without a foundation, and you can't put the roof on until you've got the walls up. There is a sequence that must be followed in order for each level of construction to be successful. With enough money to do it all, the sequencing still requires attention. You've got to have the right people to work on the foundation. There is usually a different group of people who work on the walls, electrical conduits, plumbing, and the like. The finish work calls for yet another group of artisans. Doing it all at the same time is impossible. And trying to do it all at once would inevitably lead to disaster. The same kind of sequencing is necessary in the building of a business. And remember, when the business is profitable and money is burning a hole in your pocket, don't make the Hyannis mistake. Take time for due diligence before you embark on that new adventure in growth.

On the Other Hand

Not having enough money is the more usual scenario and the first problem faced by most entrepreneurs. You can't advertise the product until the product is available. You can't sell the product without having a place to show the inventory, and the customer base to buy it. And of course, having a venue for retail sales is of no value until you've got the inventory. You ought to be getting the picture. Not having enough money, which is the usual case, requires a particular mindset. This mindset is the key to establishing the appropriate sequence and maintaining the discipline necessary to get the job done.

The Timing Problem

Hiring sales personnel and creating an advertising campaign are both seriously problematic in the new business because each represents a timing problem. As you hire salespeople, you must acknowledge that it will take some time before their efforts will result in actual sales . . . and profit. The money that you pay these people during this waiting period could be substantial. Not until the sales come rolling in will you have the profits to replenish the money already spent to develop the sales. Although each business differs depending on ordering time, delivery time, and the like, don't be surprised if it takes up to two years to catch up with the investment you've made in this activity. Similarly, as you spend money for advertising, you must recognize the obvious time hitch here as well. People don't necessarily react immediately to advertising. Experience will tell you that it generally takes multiple exposures for people to purchase, based on advertising. This is another case of advancing the money to attract customers to your service or product. For these reasons, partners must do a careful analysis of cash flow

> Advertising and sales usually demand substantial expenditures long before the resulting revenues are realized.

and be sure that their cash reservoir is sufficient to accommodate this period of investment without income.

Do you think that closure of the Hyannis nightclub may have been premature? Do you think that advertising might have generated the necessary customer base, given a longer period of time for it to achieve the goal? Do you think that the customers in the UK franchise might have come to the new location in the residential neighborhood given a longer period of time to change their buying habits? In either case, do you think it's a good idea to try to change the buying habits of a whole city . . . or a whole country?

Incremental vs. Accelerated Growth

All investors in a business, including management, must face the question of profit distribution. Most businesses have a plan for growth. Some will achieve their goal by reaching a certain point in sales and profit. In theory, the achievement of this goal might be the point at which distribution of profit becomes an alternative. The fact of the matter is that this is usually an interim goal. As a company develops strength in the marketplace, usually achieved gradually over a period of time, management will look to a different spectrum of activity for future growth. This new spectrum falls into a variety of categories. One of these is "horizontal growth," represented by opening a similar business in a different geographic area in order to establish and service an entirely new customer base. This can be done by training managers to follow the same protocols that created the original success. It can lead to a consideration of establishing a franchise operation, in which the operators of the new locations use their own money to establish the business and pay the original owner for the privilege of using the name and successful marketing methods. Another alternative is to proceed on the basis of "vertical growth," represented by creating businesses that produce the component parts or raw materials used by the business in establishing its retail product.

> Make sure you understand the language of business growth, including: vertical and horizontal growth, growth by acquisition, incremental vs. accelerated growth, outsourcing, cash vs. accrual accounting, merger, and franchising.

There is great potential for growth in either of these ways. There are also potential problems.

Growth by Acquisition

Perhaps the most aggressive growth posture is to grow by acquisition. This kind of growth is often dictated not by greed but by necessity. When the competition starts to nip at your heels, you've got to reappraise your marketing direction. If you feel that these upstarts are beginning to gnaw away at your customer base, you might consider a merger or acquisition to change the complexion of the competitive landscape.

Worksheet Questions

1. Why are advertising and sales considered to be time-sensitive problems?

2. Why is distribution of profit to shareholders unrealistic in the early days of most businesses?

3. Do you know the difference between vertical growth and horizontal growth?

4. Do you understand the concept of franchising?

5. How can competition be helpful in the growth of a new business?

6. Can the success of one company necessarily be the blueprint for successful replication of that concept?

7. Do you think that geography might play an important part in such replication?

CHAPTER 24

The Investor and the Business Plan

Goals and Expectations: "Of Course I Can Afford It"

Adam and a group of friends decided to devote some of their spare time and spare dollars to buy a piece of property for land development. They put a down payment on the property and proceeded to make monthly payments on the mortgage. Since they had no legal paperwork between them other than their signatures on the property purchase, they had essentially created a general partnership. There was no question that the property would be sought after by contractors as the town grew. But they were also aware that this was a long-term investment because of the property's location.

As months turned into a year, and as circumstances changed in each of the partners' lives, the monthly mortgage payments became more problematic for some than for others. This led to discussions, some with a bit of acrimony about selling the property before it was appropriate, just to get out from under the payment obligations.

After many months of wrangling about the questions, one of the group, Fred, had a heart attack and blamed it on the constant arguing over the property. He actually threatened to sue the partnership. Three of the partners offered to buy out his interest at a percentage of the original investment, including the payments that he had contributed to the mortgage. A short while later, as the location of the property became more desirable for development, Adam, who was leaving the community, sold his interest at a small profit to an outsider. The buyer of Adam's interest held it for another two years and eventually sold Adam's former interest at a substantial profit. His other partners were not happy about his having sold the interest to a third party instead of giving them a chance to buy it. The investment, which was expected to cement friendships, turned out to be quite a disruptive force.

❑ ❑ ❑

- Do you think that a formal, written partnership agreement with an exit strategy would have precluded many, if not all, of these problems?
- Do you think it's important for all partners to understand the goals and expectations of the other partners?
- Would you find it embarrassing to ask each partner if he or she could really afford the investment and the monthly payments? Would you ask anyway?
- Should you ask each partner to sign an affidavit to that effect?
- Do you think this affidavit would help?

The Small Investor Problem

One of the reasons that legislation has been passed to protect "the small investor" is that as time and circumstances change, the small investor may, for personal reasons, need the dollars that were invested. They may even have had in mind a more aggressive time frame that was not within the expectations of management, nor consistent with the original business plan. They want their money back! This kind of pressure on management is unfair to those others who invested their time, energy, and money, based on a plan that needed a longer time frame to succeed. It is for this very reason that you must be careful about the financial stature of the people making investments in your business. Especially family members and friends should be cautioned about the size of their investments to ensure that they don't exert this kind of pressure on management in the event of personal problems.

> Remember that the small investor as well as the large investor can become problematic in their efforts to exercise control over the future of your company.

Although it is true that an investor is a partner, the usual protocol is for this particular kind of partner to maintain a passive position in the operation of the business. This is not always the case. The more challenged the business becomes, especially in the face of financial shortfalls, the more likely it is that the silent partner will become involved. Keep in mind that although a minority shareholder of a corporation or a minority member of an LLC has no power to intrude on a business's operation, pressing problems could incite many shareholders to act in concert—a serious problem for management. By all means, try to avoid such a conundrum.

The Big Investors

Proper vetting of the investors should eliminate the problem of personal need. This does not mean, however, that the possibility of their interfering in management is eliminated. Every investor has predicated his or her investment position on the business plan presented. This business plan will have a variety of achievements that are expected to be performed or realized within specific time frames. When these time-sensitive goals are not achieved, management's control becomes vulnerable.

What Some Big Investors Are Looking For

Some investors expect their money to do phenomenal things within extraordinarily short periods of time. There are those who will tell you that they want 20 times their original investment in three to five years. You really needn't worry about these people, because the exit strategy of your business plan will usually make it crystal clear what their expectations ought to be. If they invest despite your conservative time frame, they have no basis for confrontation when their specific goals are not met. It is a good idea, however, to be sure that their expectations are similar to your own. The question of fighting for control over the destiny of your business, and your dream, needs to be resolved long before any confrontation is faced.

What Other Investors Are Looking For

Most investors have a more realistic picture of what their investment is designed to do. If you create a business plan strategy, they should recognize the time frame involved. Most investors also recognize the effect that outside influences will have over your anticipated successes, and will, up to a point, make the appropriate adjustments to their expectations, providing you satisfy them with good reasons for your changing the original plans. Most investors are looking to the longer-term results, which is the more practical view of most business ventures.

Still, as these changes become necessary, the investor groups holding a majority of shares in your company can get dangerously close to taking these prerogatives from the hands of management. When you initiate your relationship with your investors, be careful not to have any of these prerogatives available to them except, perhaps, in the most extraordinary of circumstances. This is an important aspect of the partnership relationship.

The Advantages vs. Disadvantages of an Investor Getting Involved

Although investors are usually pretty savvy people, you must be careful about the level at which you let them participate. While it is true that you don't want to forego any control of the company, keep in mind that their expertise can be tremendously helpful if it's in the nature of advisor of some sort. The idea in business is to get the very best advice from the most experienced people, then drop these nuggets into your bouillabaisse of activity. The fact of the matter is that most investors are interested in serving in some capacity on an advisory panel of some kind. It is a good policy to include these people, not only for their expertise but also to show your willingness to consider all perspectives. Unless they agree to act in concert because everything appears to be going awry, these people can be your best advisors to address not only the normal but the abnormal situations as well. There is another aspect that needs to be considered: whatever the working capital of most businesses, occasionally there is a need for additional capital. Those who are already invested in the company can be brilliant sources of new investment when and if it becomes necessary. The well-documented business plan, together with its frequent updates, is the best way to ensure that your "investor-advisors" will remain on management's side during the good days as well as the bad.

Getting the Investor in the First Place

In order to attract an investor in the first place, you must have a dream that appears to have potential, and a method of implementation that has some logical pattern of development. It is essentially the preparation of a business plan. It is appropriate, and usually mandatory, that you give some serious thought to this preparation. It is not, nor should it be, a singular document designed for a single purpose, and then discarded. A good business plan is your road map from the beginning of the journey, which involved raising the money and initiating the business, to the end of the journey, the exit strategy. It should be a document that has the flexibility to change as circumstances require, and that may be adjusted periodically to account for changes in direction when necessary and appropriate. It is your plan, developed by you, adjusted by you, and followed by you in the process of developing a successful business. Never underestimate its importance at every stage of your business's development.

"Everything Will Probably Work Out" (It Usually Won't)

It is in the best interests of every business for management to be optimistic. Keep in mind, however, that optimism in the

> You should prepare every business plan for the specific purpose you expect it to serve.

> Remember that "form" is just as important as "substance" in the preparation of a business plan.

face of disaster needs a helping hand. There seems to be a common belief in business that when left alone, most business problems will simply go away. Anyone who accepts this notion, whether in business or in everyday life, is destined for unfortunate times. While it is true that operating a business is not so complex as to prevent average people from succeeding, those who succeed are usually those who pay great attention to detail. You don't just let things happen in business; you *make them happen.*

Writing a Business Plan

Watch out for conventional wisdom! Let most of it fly over your head. You will be told that creating a business plan poses a terribly complicated problem. It doesn't. You will be told to look at a business plan format and follow it to the letter. Don't. You will be told that every part is as important as every other part. It isn't. You will be told that "substance" is the important stuff, and that "form" is not important. Wrong!

Remember the Purpose

Most business plans are designed to be a tool by which management can monitor the growth of a business. A plan will enable you to periodically do a comparative analysis to see which ideas worked in the past and which didn't. You will be able to increase and maximize your efforts by examining and reexamining the most cost-effective ways to grow. There are, of course, other purposes to be served as well. You might intend the business plan to be used for enticing a company to enter into a joint venture with you. You might want to use it to convince a bank that your company would be a good lending risk. You might want to excite an investor group to invest in your company because it has an exciting future.

You'll notice that one generic business plan is not likely to satisfy all of the above purposes. In order to serve each goal, you will need to adjust each business plan to fulfill the likely needs of the reader. And you've got to make it interesting enough for the reader to get excited about reading it in the first place.

What the Package Should Look Like

Make your business plan colorful, clear, and concise. Form is every bit as important as substance. If the reader can't read it easily, your entire purpose goes down the drain. Don't try to put 100 words in a space that is only big enough for 50. Use bullets for emphasis and enough space between lines to allow for easy reading. Don't use anything less than 12-point type, and don't use some exotic font that makes it difficult to read. Don't use words that only you or your peers will understand. Remember that the reader is not likely to know as much about your business as you do. Use pictures, color logos, and the like . . . without going overboard. Don't get wordy and expect the reader to enjoy your prose. That's not the purpose of the exercise.

Don't Ask Someone Else to Build the Plan

Aside from the fact that you must understand the business plan for your own purposes, you will likely have to face questions from the reader at some point. It would be foolish to have someone else prepare the plan and then have you fall on your face when you don't understand what it says. You need to understand the most significant features of your business, assigning to them the appropriate priority placement for the benefit of the reader and the purpose you've designed the plan to serve. Only you can create these building blocks. Then, after getting some feedback on readability from people who understand your business—and from people who don't—you might ask an editor to ensure that the grammar, punctuation, and syntax are in good order.

The Most Significant Parts

While every business has its peculiarities, the two most important features in most business plans are the marketing and the financials. Every reader wants to know that you understand your competitive position in the marketplace and that you have built your business in such a way that it will enable you to prosper. Because the presentation of your business plan is usually for the purpose of getting something from the reader, it is important for you to understand the financial paperwork that shows the current, or future, financial success of the

The investor must be satisfied that you understand your financial paperwork as well as your position in the competitive business marketplace.

company. Always keep in mind that you don't have to be an accountant, a lawyer, or a marketing guru to write a good business plan. If that were the case, then the American small-business landscape would be naked. And you know that this is not the case. Learn what you need to learn in order to understand the nature of the competitive marketplace and your financial needs. And don't forget, no one is likely to grasp the nuances of your business better than you do.

What Should It Look Like?

The following is designed to suggest the kind of language that may be used in each of the basic areas in the average business plan. Each product or service, depending on its position in the competitive marketplace, will clearly involve a different use of language and will require more time on some aspects than on others. Remember always that the devil is in the details. Don't leave out the answers to significant questions and, at the same time, don't bore the reader to death with minutia that will not lead them to the success picture you're trying to paint. If you have statistics or charts that you feel might be significant to some readers but boring to others, make a note in your narrative that they can be found in the Appendix or Addenda at the close of the plan. In this way, the reader who wants to move on will not be slowed down, and the reader who wants the specifics will not be disappointed.

All right, what does a business plan actually look like? Since every presentation needs an introduction, you will find what is called an executive summary at the beginning of every business plan.

The purpose of the executive summary is to say hello, make the appropriate introductions, explain the purpose, and set the stage for the proposal of the plan. It may be to borrow money, to interest people in becoming a part of the company, etc. It is important to note that the executive summary should be prepared before the actual plan is written. This is to ensure that you have developed the appropriate focus in your own mind. *When you get through putting the actual pieces of the plan together, you should then be prepared to rewrite the executive summary.* You will find that the second time around, you will have developed a somewhat different focus from the one you started with. This is perfectly appropriate. In fact, it's preferable because your own perspective will have changed as a result of reading what you know the recipient of the plan will be reading.

Executive Summary

Since it is always best to personalize your presentation and to move quickly to explain what's involved, note the suggestions that follow:

Dear Charles and Charlene: *(Try to personalize however and whenever you can. Make sure you spell their names correctly.)*

There is a great opportunity to establish a competitive position in the business of . . .

(The words "competitive position" tell the reader that you understand the reality of competition.)

The nature of our business is to offer a product (a service) superior to our competition in quality and value.

(This is where you need to be creative, succinct, and dynamic.)

With my personal education, background, and experience, I understand the nature of the industry and the methods by which such a business can be exciting and successful . . .

(You have now told the reader that you are not a novice and have "the goods" to establish a successful business.)

I have established a group of people whose experience in the field will leave no stone unturned . . .

(It is important for the reader to know that you are not acting alone, but in concert with an experienced and talented team.)

The growth plan requires an investment of $XXX, and the projections that follow should give you every confidence that the break-even point and profit position will be achieved as anticipated . . .

(This will clarify what you are looking for, qualify the reader to some extent, and—one would hope—cause the reader to examine the financials to see if your plan is achievable.)

The investment gives the investor the opportunity to own a piece of the equity in the long term and enjoy the return of most of the investment in the short term . . .

(Although explained in a previous chapter, this feature allows an investor to have some of his or her investment returned as a loan, with the remainder represented by an equity position in the company. It attracts many investors with an interesting combination of loan and investment.)

I invite you to read the following material and ask any questions you may have.

Cordially,

Entrepreneur

Management and Outsourcing

You will note that I referenced certain people in the Executive Summary and you will have an opportunity to examine their credentials. Outside legal analysis has also established the appropriate legal protections where applicable: copyright, trademark, patent.

(The mere appearance of other people involved presents a serious comfort zone for many, if not most, investors. It's also a good idea to reference your use of outside legal help to ensure the appropriate protection of proprietary information.)

The Product and a Competitive Analysis

You will note the sources of raw material as well as component parts:

- Our competitive position in the marketplace including the pricing differentials.
- Our unique product features and legally protected position, where applicable.

- The growth potential of the product, including the collateral and after-market opportunities available after the initial success is achieved (complementary products, distribution alternatives, etc.). You will note the actual competitive analysis done in the form of a matrix, showing how our product and distribution are superior to the existing methods of the competition.

  (Very few things are as important to your business plan as having your reader understand that you completely understand competitive analysis of your product or service and the niche position you expect to achieve in the competitive marketplace.)

The Marketing Plan

You will note the various methods of advertising and free promotion available to us and the time line developed for utilization of each. You will note the customer profile and the particular market niche that we've developed in order to challenge the competition with our own specialization.

(You will always be well served by explaining the research you've done on your prospective customer base, and how you expect to approach it.)

The Financials

You will note that we have put together Profit and Loss Statements for the first three years as well as Cash Flow Forecasts for the same period. This will enable you to recognize the dollar utilization and the return of capital within the designated time parameters. Please note specifically the Assumptions that are attributable to each of the line items and the time frames involved. These Assumptions, together with the Balance Sheets, have been carefully examined and analyzed to present a fair and accurate appraisal of the company's continuing financial stability as well as its growth potential.

(It is important to emphasize the use of "Assumptions" and necessary for the reader to understand that the financials represent a "narrative of numbers." Without the appropriate Assumptions, it is difficult, if not impossible, to interpret the numbers to your advantage.)

Operations

In addition to the specific expertise of the people listed, you will note that the company is represented by just that number of qualified people to ensure that we will reach each plateau according to the plan. You will also note the contingency arrangements in the event that each plateau is not reached within the designated time frames.

> Make sure that you use the necessary assumptions to help explain the bare numbers of your financial paperwork.

(The reader must be able to recognize your ability to change direction in the event of unexpected circumstances. You must show that this "adjustment" would not prevent the company from achieving its goals.)

Exit Strategy

With success potential at various levels, depending on time, the economy, and the proper utilization of investment dollars, we have structured a variety of methods by which every investor may enjoy the benefits of the company's success. These include alternatives for return OF investment as well as return ON investment. We look forward to the optimum opportunities that come with growth, including the possibility of franchising, merger with a larger company, and the potential of an Initial Public Offering.

(Note that the idea of "loan and investment" has been reiterated here in other language to ensure that the investor knows you can be flexible in negotiating a final agreement.)

The above does not represent every aspect of every business plan; each business will have its own special needs and nuances. It should, however, give you a handle on the approach that businesses have found to be successful. A variety of business plan formats are available on the internet. Be careful about following them too closely. Too little information is obviously deficient. Too much information is surplus, and can be distracting. Make sure you include all that is necessary and appropriate.

Worksheet Questions

1. Do you think that form is as important as substance in a business plan?

2. How can management use the business plan as a tool to monitor the growth of a business?

3. Why should you not ask someone else to prepare your business plan?

4. Why should you put most of your complex charts and graphs at the end of your business plan?

5. Why should you try to personalize your business plan to each recipient?

6. Do you think there is truth in the adage, "Investors are more interested in a weak product with a strong team than a strong product with a weak team"?

7. Why is the use of assumptions important in the financial section of your plan?

8. What is the primary problem with small investors?

9. Why should you avoid industry jargon in your business plan?

10. Do you think your investors want to know that you understand your competitive position in the marketplace?

Selling the Business

To the Clone or the Big Guy?

Bringing an Employee/Partner into an Existing Business

Eleanor Spindell had an interesting conundrum. She had built a successful discount mailer business by being very aggressive in her selling campaign. She was getting ready to sell the business but was aware of two things: that the business would likely be sold with a down payment and with the balance of the purchase price to be paid over a period of years, and that the buyer would need to be extremely sales-oriented in order for the business to grow, let alone survive. She therefore wanted to make sure that the buyer would not only be a capable salesperson but would also have a substantial enough business to protect its continuity and, in turn, to protect the payments on the balance of the purchase price. She was not greedy, but she wanted to be careful to protect the equity she had built.

One very sales-oriented buyer, James Galbraith, appeared as a likely candidate and, after substantial discussion, an agreement was reached. It was a somewhat unique scenario but made sense to both parties. James would take a job with Eleanor to sell additional space. The current advertising revenue was based on 35 spaces already sold, but the "package" had an opportunity for 35 more spaces as a result of recent changes in publishing capability. James would keep all the net revenue from the spaces he sold and would have the option to buy the business in 18 months based on the value of the business when he started. This way, he would not be paying for a value that he, himself, helped build. His selling would not increase the price when he was ready to buy.

Note the mutual benefits that this relationship afforded:

- James could earn as much as $100,000 per year if he sold the maximum of 35 additional spaces.
- He could double the size (and the value) of the business but would pay only what the business was worth when he started.
- Eleanor would get the full value for the equity she earned in the business she built.
- James would have a business so substantial when he bought it that he would be incentivized to protect it for a long time, eventually selling it to someone else at another profit.
- Eleanor would be assured of receiving the balance of the purchase price.

This plan could just as easily have been accomplished by having James buy into the business as a partner and still have the option to buy the balance of the company later on. But because James did not have the down payment to do this, the alternative scenario of being a nonlegal partner accomplished that purpose for both parties. Neither James nor Eleanor had anything to lose and both had something to gain—a win-win situation. It is essentially a partnership without being a partnership at all. In its practical application, however, it is a partnership relationship in many ways.

It Should be "In the Works" the Day You Start Your Business

Every business plan, regardless of the purpose for which it was designed, includes a section called an "exit strategy." This section can refer to how a lender will be able to have a loan returned; it might be a projection of how an equity partner will ultimately see a multiple of his or her original investment; or it could describe the method by which the business will devolve to a family member, or merely how the business will be sold.

Value as a Secondary Issue

There are a myriad of ways that investors as well as management can get a return of and on their investment. The method by which this is designed to happen and the time line that it follows are very important elements in every business plan and should be a prerequisite for every partnership relationship. It is inevitable that in every business relationship there will come a time when one or another of the partners will have changed his or her expectations and goals for the future. Sometimes it is as simple as the creating, building, and growing of a family. Sometimes it results from tragedy in a family. In still other cases, it is as simple as a change in priorities as one partner grows older. And selling the business is the ultimate exit strategy.

To many entrepreneurs, the valuation of the business, the establishment of a selling price, is the highest priority. Many sellers, after the fact, recognize valuation as the least of their problems. Although there are people who will tell you how complex the issue of valuation is and how expensive it can be, the reality is that valuating a small business is relatively simple and need not be expensive at all. The real problem is how to structure the sale of the business, regardless of price. As so often is the case, the devil is in the details, and woe to those who lose sight of this very important warning.

The Buyer: An All-Important Element

Whatever the details of the sale, the most important aspect is the buyer, that buyer's integrity, the reasons for the purchase, and a variety of other personal factors that many sellers consider unimportant. Since most small businesses are sold with the seller "holding paper" for the balance of the purchase price, the buyer's financial status and whatever additional security may be available should be a high priority. The buyer's background, together with his or her reputation in the community, can turn out to be a subtle reason to reconsider the buyer as a candidate. Although the buyer with the biggest purse is usually the one in whom sellers are most interested, this also must be taken with a grain of salt. After all, if you're going to be "the banker" and hold a purchase money promissory note, a promissory note for the balance of the purchase price, the buyer's purse is only an indication of his or her ability to pay; it doesn't necessarily reflect a willingness to adhere to the terms and conditions of the sale.

A Likely Candidate Right at Home

This is one of the reasons why a key employee who doesn't have the requisite dollars you're looking for may still be the best candidate you can find in the long run. This is a person you've learned to trust who has a real understanding of proper business operation, and who may be willing to listen to your advice during the period of transition—and beyond. Your employee is not necessarily the only worthy candidate, but is certainly worth careful consideration before you make a decision. Also, don't discount the candidate's ability to raise additional capital. He or she may have an aunt or uncle who has been waiting to help this niece or nephew along the way.

Assessing the Risk

Is the buyer taking the purchase seriously? When the business is a franchise, the seller can expect the franchisor to vet the buyer, at least to the extent of discovering his or her capabilities to learn and understand the basics of the business. There is usually a mandatory training period given by the franchisor to ensure that the buyer understands the basic tools by which to operate the business. In a nonfranchise situation, it is incumbent upon the seller to stay with the business during a transition period after the sale. This will, one hopes, ensure that the buyer is qualified to operate the business, has an understanding of the subtleties involved, and evidences a feeling for the underlying nuances of the business. In the final analysis, if you're going to be holding a promissory note representing the balance of the purchase price, you must recognize that you are accepting part of the risk of the buyer's ability to at least maintain the business that you've built . . . until the note is paid.

A Word about the Franchise

In the event that you are a franchisee and selling your franchise, you ought to keep two things in mind. The first is that the franchise company cannot put itself in the middle of a potential sale. It would be a serious conflict of interest and conceivably cause the franchisor considerable legal problems after the sale. The second thing is that the franchise company is interested in perpetuating the franchise and would, logically, be more concerned about the buyer than the seller, because the seller will be out of the picture. Carefully weigh any advice you get from the franchisor in light of the long-term involvement that the company will have with the buyer.

This is not denigrating the franchisor; it is merely acknowledging that in every business dealing, each party has priorities that will not necessarily coincide with the priorities of the others. A franchise exists by its royalties; the royalties depend on the continued success of the existing locations; and this success depends in great part on the initiative and incentive of the owners. These are the areas in which the franchisor must exercise its greatest effort. It is true that the reputation of the franchisor depends on many things, including the facility of transitioning ownership. Most people, however, understand that the success or failure of this transition is attributable to the seller, as well as to the franchisor.

The Flesh and the Skeleton

Many sellers feel that the security they need to support the sale and to protect the balance of the purchase price can be the business itself. This is perhaps the biggest mistake that a seller can make. In the first place, most sellers have no intention of returning to the business once it is sold. In the second place, it

> After taking a down payment, be sure that you have adequate security to protect against any default in the payment of the balance of the purchase price.

doesn't take long for a bad buyer, inadvertently or intentionally, to completely destroy a business that might have taken the seller years to build. You may end up taking back the business and find that it is a mere skeleton of the business you sold, and with more obligations than when you left. Taking back the business is not an option. You need additional security to protect the promissory note you hold for the balance of the purchase price. Walking away with only the down payment in hand is hardly the result that the seller expects. Yet, often, this is the case when the seller fails to recognize the vulnerability of taking on part of the risk without exercising the appropriate cautions.

Different Kinds of Security

Most buyers will bring a certain amount of cash to the table. It is unusual for a buyer to pay all in cash. Buyers are usually advised, in fact, not to pay all cash because they lose any leverage they might have to protect against misrepresentations made by the seller, whether intentional or otherwise. It is true that a buyer may borrow from another source, a lending institution, sometimes guaranteed by the Small Business Administration, and they will have to pay back this loan instead of a "loan" from the seller. In most cases, the buyer will have this obligation to someone. Because most businesses carry a certain degree of risk, most lending institutions are not keen to offer the bulk of the money needed to buy the business, and will usually want the seller to retain some risk for the same reason: potential misrepresentations or bad management.

What Other Security?

Additional security usually comes in the form of a guarantor, someone of substantial financial stature who is willing to stand behind the buyer, essentially putting their own assets at risk. It can also be an equity position in a piece of property, usually the equity in the buyer's home or other property. This puts the buyer much more at risk and ought to put the seller's mind much more at ease.

The second mortgage or second trust deed may not even represent a substantial equity position in the property. But it has its consequences. Before the owner can refinance or sell the property, the holder of the second mortgage will need to be paid off. These implications are serious enough to be effective on the seller's behalf.

Thinking about Tomorrow

One of the last items of consequence, which really ought to be one of the first, is that the seller must think about what tomorrow may bring, after the sale is consummated. Many sellers, wanting to get out of the entrepreneurial box due to frustration or other personal motives, fail to consider that after the business is sold, their incomes will not be as substantial as when they were in business. In fact, when the payment schedule on the promissory note for the balance of the purchase price is finished, there will be no income at all. "Life after sale" is seldom given enough mature and careful thought. Don't be guilty of this in your own situation. Any business broker or business consultant worth his or her salt will usually bring this up at your first meeting. And they will usually insist on meeting both husband and wife or significant other to ensure that this all-important element is discussed by all affected parties. This also means that meeting with only one partner is bad protocol. Failure to do this might suggest that the consultant is more interested in his or her fee than in your welfare. It's a good litmus test of the ethical stature of the professional in whom you repose trust and confidence relative to your family and your future.

Monitoring the Buyer

As long as there are monies still owed to the seller, he or she has the prerogative, indeed, the obligation, to monitor the ongoing business after the sale. Looking at the buyer's profit-and-loss statements, balance sheets, and tax payments will give you an idea as to how safe and secure the balance of your payments will be. Should you notice glitches in the financials, you might be able to help stabilize the business if the buyer is making mistakes in judgment—assuming, of course, that he or she is willing to listen. There are many instances in which the purchase-and-sale agreement will call for a cap on the buyer's compensation as long as money is still owed to the seller. This, of course, is just the tip of the iceberg of protective measures available to the cautious seller. Make sure you examine these and other protections before closing the door on the sale. Remember, once you've established a price for your business, the buyer has most of the negotiating prerogatives. Don't give up the few you have left without a careful analysis.

A Plethora of Candidates

What is most interesting is that the typical candidates are still out there looking. And they are not the only ones. There is a younger group, whose members feel that their energy and innovative ideas represent the baseline for accelerated growth. And there is the older group of candidates who feel that their practical experience in the industry will give them a leg up in growing a business. There are many who don't want to answer to others because they feel their business judgment is better than the judgment of their employers. Others want to build something for their children. A common desire is to be the "captain of my ship and the master of my destiny." But now there is a new group of people for whom there is no alternative but to be in business for themselves. They have been in industry with good jobs and good pay and good benefits . . . and now the job is gone. They have been downsized. The jobs that are available neither use their experience and abilities nor generate the kind of money that they are used to. Most of these people have some money that they have saved over the years or that represents their "golden parachute," but they know that it will not last unless they put it to good use. These people comprise the new group in addition to the usual suspects.

Buying an Existing Business

Although many think about starting a new business, others recognize that buying an existing business eliminates a great deal of the gamble involved in starting from scratch. They understand that the history of an existing business can be a pretty good gauge of its future if many of the basic business elements can be maintained. A business that is capable of generating an immediate income, even though it might not be capable of generating a rocketing dot-com-type growth, can be very appealing to someone who needs to create a comfort zone for the family and the future. The only caution is to be certain that you understand the nature of the business, its position in the industry of which it is a part, and the place that it has in the competitive marketplace.

A good concept to keep in mind is that "a business ought to be able to buy itself." In other words, once the buyer puts a substantial down payment on the shop, the buyer's compensation as well as payments to the seller or whomever else has loaned the money for the purchase should come from the profit of the business. With this in mind, many qualified people will be willing, if not anxious, to be among the buyer candidate group.

Negotiating Too Hard

For whatever reason, both the buyer and the seller of a business each feel that they must have the upper hand during negotiations. This usually applies to all the documentation of a sale as well as its price and terms. Those who have had enough experience will tell you that this need not be the case. The deal that is consummated must meet the reasonable requirements of both parties. The price must be such that the business can buy itself. The terms must be such that the seller can enjoy the equity that's been earned while the buyer can enjoy the benefits of ownership and profit sufficient to feed the family. Last but not least is the fact that the paperwork must allow both sides to feel comfortably protected. The seller must have some assurance of collecting the balance of the purchase price, and the buyer must have some assurance that the business is what the seller represented it to be.

Do You Want a "Clone" or a "Big Guy"?

If a company that is larger than yours buys your business, it is likely that it will have a cadre of people who can assemble all the talent needed to maintain and build the business. Selling to a clone is different in many ways. It is essentially selling to someone very much like yourself. This person will undoubtedly have some specific talents but will likely lack other business skills. No one person constitutes the perfect package of all the talents necessary to successfully operate a business. You will need to assess these talents—those that are apparent and those that are apparently absent. Keep in mind that most businesses are not sold for cash but rather for a down payment, the balance of the purchase price being paid over a period of time. You will need to scrutinize the buyer's talents in terms of his or her ability to maintain the continuity of the business. Your ability to collect the balance of the purchase price might well be at risk. Security for the balance is a must, but it shouldn't take the place of a competent buyer.

The Numbers Must Speak for You

It's easy to let your paperwork take a backseat when you are in charge of the business on a daily basis. After all, you know just what your break-even point is, what sales are necessary to keep the boat afloat, and what expenses will allow you to have spending money at the end of the month. Any buyer will want the comfort of knowing all these things, and more, and will not likely be willing to accept your representations without the proof of real numbers that have substance behind them. Start working on your books long before you anticipate presenting them to a buyer candidate. Speak to a professional consultant to be sure that the numbers you are preparing are the kinds of numbers normally sought by a buyer.

> Be sure to have your financial paperwork properly prepared before putting your business up for sale.

Every Buyer Is Looking for Something Special

Every business, even in the same industry, is going to be different. One business might have an extraordinary capability in the kind of work it can produce or the time in which the work can be processed. Another business may have a top-notch sales force that can maintain the business in the face of substantial competition or even in the face of a soft economy. And some businesses are maintained at a minimal cost, in terms of facility rent, personnel, or equipment that is completely paid for. Identify just what exceptional business feature *you* have to offer. It might very well dictate the kind of buyers you ought to be looking for. After all, each of them is looking for some specific advantages that might make the difference in the competitive marketplace.

Start Early with the Most Logical Candidates

When it comes to buyer-candidate selection, you must do your homework. If you have a business that depends on a particular geographic area for your customer base, you will likely want to consider a buyer who is already in that area. If it's a big guy, the proximity might very well be a positive factor. If it's a clone, his or her familiarity with the territory could also be advantageous.

Don't wait until you need to sell to start your interview process. And that's exactly what it is—an interview process. The best time to sell is when you don't have to. Remember the old saying about banks: "They are more likely to lend you money when you don't need it." Start your interview process on a positive note: "When the time is right, I'd like to consider selling my business and I want to make sure that its future is in the right hands." Start by inviting the CEO or the entrepreneur to lunch. Keep it on a casual basis. You'd be surprised what will come out in a casual conversation when you are candid in your approach. The advertising and usual business-broker approach can be left until much later. The personal touch, as with most endeavors, will usually prove to be the most effective.

Start Planning Long Before You Start Selling

A buyer is going to want to see a business that can stand on its own. They don't want to see a business that is shaky in areas of equipment, computer technology, or even personnel. They want to see a business to which the seller has devoted his or her best efforts. Buyers have no interest in hearing that "the business could be bigger if we had paid more attention to our advertising." They will usually wonder why you didn't. Nor are prospects excited to learn that "many more dollars could have been generated if certain things had been attended to." The buyer will usually wonder why you didn't do this either. In other words, don't make excuses for the things you could have done and should have done prior to putting the business on the market. This is almost as bad as telling the buyer that all the sales are not necessarily recorded for one reason or another and that, actually, the sales picture is much larger than it appears to be. If a buyer thinks that you've "shorted" the government on sales taxes, they will naturally wonder what else is less than honest in your presentation. Remember that selling is negotiating, and negotiating is based almost entirely on credibility. Don't lose your credibility at the beginning of your relationship. You'll never get it back! And always remember: you don't get a second chance to make a first impression.

The Asset Sale vs. the Stock Sale

A business can be sold by transferring ownership of the company, represented by the equity or the outstanding shares of stock, or it can be sold by transferring ownership of the assets. These are two entirely different approaches to the sale of a business and you must understand the difference. If you buy the shares of stock in the company, you essentially buy the entire box of assets together with everything over the box, under the box, and around the box. You may be inheriting legal problems that even the seller is unaware of. The tax implications for the seller are somewhat less onerous, but the buyer may be buying much more than was ever anticipated. If you choose to do this, for whatever reasons, you should be sure that you have the right to withhold or offset payments on the balance owed on the purchase price in the event that something unexpected happens. The least you should do is to put some of the purchase price into an escrow account for a sufficient period of time to handle the unexpected.

Be sure to have your signature and that of your spouse or significant other removed from all obligations before finalizing your sale.

The more conventional purchase would be an asset purchase in which you buy the things specified in your bill of sale. This may include the name of the business as well as inventory, all physical assets, and proprietary information, all of which are specifically noted. Any question of the tax implications can always be resolved by adjusting the purchase price.

The Last—and Biggest—Concern

When you sell a business, be sure that you have removed yourself from all the ongoing obligations of the business: the lease for the premises, the leases on the equipment purchases, the bank loans for the purchase of equipment. If you leave your name on these obligations, you may be liable for them long after the buyer destroys the business and goes on his or her way. And remember what contracts are all about. They are not created for the dishonest. They are created to eliminate ambiguity and provide the antidote to bad memory. If somebody "wants to get ya, they'll get ya." This is why, even with a good contract in place, you must understand the motives of the buyer and have a clear picture as to whether his or her goals are the same for the business as were yours.

Worksheet Questions

1. To what degree do you think that the integrity of the buyer is an important consideration?

2. Which do you think is more important, the buyer's financial stature or the buyer's integrity?

3. Do you understand that most small businesses are not sold for cash?

4. Do you think it's a good idea to consider your key employees as prospective buyer candidates, even if they don't appear to have all the dollars needed to buy?

5. Why is a training period essential after the sale if you are carrying the balance of the purchase price?

6. Do you know why many people consider buying an existing business rather than starting their own?

7. Do you know the advantages and the disadvantages of selling to a clone?

8. Why should you be careful about removing your name from all obligations at the time of sale?

The Phantom Partnership

Half Now and "Maybe" Half Later

Alfred Martinez and his father, Alonzo, went to a business consultant seeking help in acquiring an orthodontics practice. Alfred, a practicing dentist, had just finished his graduate work and was ready to start this new phase of his professional life. Alonzo had found a practice in Truth or Consequences, New Mexico, and wanted the consultant to accompany him to further the negotiations. When they arrived, they met the orthodontist and his broker.

The Broker's Representations

The price for the business was essentially agreed upon; however, there was a glitch. It is understood in the dental profession that about one-half of the business developed in an orthodontist's practice derives from the recommen-dations of existing clients. This was not a problem, as Alonzo knew that the quality of his son's work would make this happen. The other half of the orthodontist's clientele, however, comes from the referrals of local dentists. Since the buyer would be moving into this new neighbor-hood as a stranger, the chances of this happening would appear to be slim because he had no existing relationship with the dental community there.

The Guarantee

To assuage this apparent concern, the seller's broker explained, "This will not be a problem. Once my client (the seller) embraces your client (the buyer) in a manner of speaking, he will automatically *inherit* the total package of the dentists' referrals." Although this comment was likely made in good faith, the reality of the relationships between the seller and the other den-tists, predicated on poker games, bowling, school ties, and the like, made this "guarantee" less than comforting in the mind of the buyer.

A Different Approach

The buyer's consultant suggested that since the seller's broker was so sure of the buyer inheriting the dentists' referrals, a simple solution might be in order. For the one-half of the business that was predicated on the buyer's ability to inspire his own patients to make recommendations, the agreed upon purchase price would be paid in cash. For the other half of the business that depended on the dentists' recommendations (which the broker had been so quick to guarantee), that part of the price for the business would be paid incrementally, every six months for two years based on a particular formula. It would be based on the number of referrals actually received by the buyer, relative to the number actually received by the seller in the same six-month period of the previous year. In that way, the seller would receive the entire purchase price if the dentists' recommendations were consistent with the seller's history. If the percentage was only one-third, then the seller would receive only one-third of the second half of the purchase price during that two-year period. The seller's broker went ballistic and accused the consultant of not knowing what he was doing. In other words, this suggestion did not fall on receptive ears. After a short tirade on the issue by the seller's broker, the buyer suggested to his consult-ant that they return home.

The Phantom Partnership

The following month, Alonzo and the consultant met with a local orthodontist and the very same conversation took place. The seller's answer was, "That makes a lot of sense. And to be sure that we maximize our efforts to deliver those referrals, I will stay with the business as a visible partner for a while so that both the dentists and the patients will have some comfort in the transition." By creating a partnership of sorts, the sale was consummated to the advantage of both buyer and seller. Alfred has, since the purchase, enjoyed a very successful practice as an orthodontist. And the seller received full value for the equity he earned.

Sale of a Professional Practice by Creating a Phantom Partnership

The sale of a professional practice could be very problematic, because the loyalty between doctor and patient is not easily transferred to a buyer. A partnership can be a practical way to keep the loyalty of the customer base with the actual takeover at a later date. It is a good idea for a variety of reasons. With a phantom partnership, in which a legal partnership has not actually been formed, the clientele feel that

> A phantom partnership is the key to the successful sale of a professional business.

there is an addition to the office rather than a deletion. And even though many clients or patients will actually be serviced by the new "partner," the feeling of continuity is a comfort zone for most of them. In addition, the attempt by the seller of the practice to maximize the transfer of clients and referrals to the buyers during this interim period can be very effective for both parties.

Although the question of loyalty and the ability to transfer that loyalty from seller to buyer was not nearly as difficult for Eleanor Spindell in Chapter 25, the same concept prevails. The idea of the customer or patient seeing an *addition* to the firm rather than a subtraction is a perfect solution to the problem. There will be those detractors who contend that this is a deceptive practice because the customers are being misled. The fact of the matter is that this arrangement allows the customer to maintain continuity with confidence if the buyer turns out to be just as competent as the seller. The customer always retains the right to leave and choose a different purveyor or professional. Yes, it is a ploy, but it is designed to be positive, not negative or destructive in any way. Think of the many different kinds of businesses to which this concept of the phantom partnership is applicable:

- The massage therapist
- The personal chef
- The business consultant
- The personal trainer
- Veterinarians
- Insurance brokers
- Counselors of all sorts
- Teachers
- Accountants and lawyers
- Physicians of all types

The Business Valuation

The reason for having an exit strategy, which is not a high priority at the beginning of most business ventures, usually involves the potential for change in the goals and expectations of the parties as a business grows. Sometimes it is the result of the owner moving on to greener pastures, or the fact that the business has, under this owner's auspices, achieved its highest plateau of success. It may also be that the owner wants to retire and the sale of the business will enable him or her to achieve this new goal. Sometimes it is the result of inquiry by other companies interested in acquisition for growth purposes. Whatever the reasons, the need to value the business properly is an essential element in the activity. Equally important are decisions about how best to grow the equity of the business before putting it on the market. This will ensure a higher price for the business. A periodic business valuation will give you the tools you need. A periodic comparative analysis will highlight the actions that helped build the equity, and those things that were not as productive.

> Acquisition timing is important to the growth path of your business.

The Equipment Conundrum

Building equity in a business involves more than a single item. It involves the need for new equipment to maintain the business's competitive position in the marketplace. Timing must also be taken into account because such a purchase will, for some time, negatively affect the value of the business. It is the question of the cart before the horse. You can't pull the cart without the horse but, without the cart, the horse will be of minimal value. When you acquire equipment, it could be because you already have a customer base that can only be satisfied if you have what is necessary to produce their product. In some cases, a business will acquire the equipment, hoping that its availability will enable the company to attract a bigger customer base. Any such approach must be coupled with the ability of the owner to pay for the equipment as the customer base is being generated.

> Expenses against revenues are a key to the valuation of a business.

Expenses Against Revenues

In the latter case, payments for the equipment will usually outpace the development of customer growth. During this growth period, when your marketing accentuates the new equipment capability, the cost of the equipment will not be equaled by the customer business generated, and will be an additional "expense against revenues." Since bottom-line profit is the basis of valuing the equity of a company, this premature acquisition of equipment will shrink the bottom line and lower the value of the business. This does not mean the acquisition should not be made. It merely means that the partners must weigh the cost against the potential revenues and, especially, the effect such an acquisition may have on the value of the business in the event that the partners are anticipating an imminent sale. This is exactly why a business plan and a periodic valuation of every business should be part of your written goals and expectations.

Worksheet Questions

1. Why is timing so important in the acquisition of equipment in a business?

2. Why is the acquisition problematic in the short term and advantageous in the long term?

3. Why is this question of acquisition timing important to an exit strategy?

4. What do expenses against revenues have to do with business valuation?

5. Why is it important to value your partnership periodically?

6. Why is it important to examine an exit strategy at the beginning of a partnership?

7. Why should partners continually examine their individual goals and expectations?

8. What is a phantom partnership?

9. How can a phantom partnership help in the sale of a professional practice?

10. Why is it important for each partner to understand the needs and expectations of the other?

11. Why is adjusting your expectations the key to partnership success?

CHAPTER 27

Bringing in New Partners

The Equity Split

When Ten Fingers Just Aren't Enough

Mark Bitner had started a graphics business and had, after three years, established a solid customer base and a successful business. He realized, however, that his future growth was severely limited since all the work, in addition to selling his product and spending time on marketing and financial paperwork, was being done by him. He also realized that in order to build the business and take it to the next plateau of success and profit, he would need to hire someone to work with him.

Going It Alone Has Its Limitations

In his search for a working associate, he was fortunate to find someone with equal experience in the business and someone who wanted to be a long-term contributor to this business. Jason Marsh had been working for various people in the industry but was interested in owning a business of his own. He realized that a job would always be a job, and that his future income was limited to the discretion of the people he worked for. He didn't have the money to invest in all the equipment for a new business and was looking for an existing one in which he might become a partner. As serendipity would have it, Mark and Jason came together. Jason took the job with a partnership view to the future.

What Does Percentage of Ownership Really Mean?

Jason proved to be a substantial asset to the business. And Mark agreed that he wanted Jason as his partner, as much for the stability of Jason's future as for Mark's own future and their business. Mark and Jason decided to get a valuation of the business in order to determine the percentage of ownership that Jason's available capital could buy. Some very interesting things happened. The first thing was that Jason and Mark arbitrarily agreed that Jason's limited capital of $5,000 was worth about 5 percent of the business, based on an arbitrary business valuation of $100,000. This arbitrary valuation was in Mark's mind and came from a gut feeling. Interestingly, Mark had purchased some expensive equipment during the year, which increased the capability of the business in the long term but detracted from the valuation of the business in the short term. The valuation was done by a professional who found that, as a result of the recent acquisition of this equipment, the business was worth significantly less than the $100,000 picked by Mark as the business's value. It is interesting to note that had the business been valued before the purchase of the new equipment, Mark's figure might have been quite realistic. The payments on the new equipment were additional expenses against revenues and lowered the operating profit on which the valuation was based. All of this coincided with the hiring of Jason. This problem is discussed in much greater detail in Chapter 28 on business valuations.

The Conundrum

Even though Mark and Jason had agreed to 5 percent for $5,000, the problem was that the valuation did not reflect the basis for that agreement. It was clear that these two prospective partners, who had worked together for a year, knew that this partnership was already a successful working relationship and they didn't want to lose it. The synergy of the two of them had already increased the business substantially and confirmed the definition of synergy as 2 + 2 = 9. They also recognized that their agreement would likely have reflected the actual value at the time Jason joined the company and before the new equipment was purchased.

The Solution

Although it had already been agreed that Jason's salary would be increased significantly, the question of percentage of ownership was still unresolved. It was up to the parties to find the right path to resolution. It was subsequently agreed that the $5,000 would still buy the 5 percent of the business but that the distribution of any profit at the end of the year would give 20 percent of the profit, not 5 percent of the profit, to Jason. This was based on the fact that the anticipated growth of the business would certainly be due, in great part, to Jason's participation in the business and the resulting contribution from the added customer base. Mark was in agreement with this position and the problem was solved to the benefit of both parties. The lesson to be learned from this story is that the answer is not always in the numbers alone.

Every entrepreneur realizes, some earlier than others, that he or she is not able to take the business to the next plateau of success without an infusion of capital, technical experience, industry relationships, sales capability, or merely the addition of another ten fingers. When this happens, the question of hiring or partnering invariably arises. Even though the business might have already achieved a modicum of success, the reinvesting of operating profit often tends to minimize the value of the business at that time. As a result, a new partner in the business might get a greater or smaller percentage of the business, depending on the negotiating position of the parties. There are many variables involved in these equations. The best suggestion is to get good advice on negotiating alternatives.

Maintaining Control

Before examining questions of percentages relative to the value of a business, every entrepreneur needs to face the question of giving up control. It is

Make sure you understand the level of control you are ceding or assuming in your partnership arrangement based on your percentage of equity participation.

important to keep in mind that an entrepreneur usually develops a business out of a dream. In order to fulfill that dream, he or she must be free to develop the time line that is appropriate to the best interests of the business and to his or her expectations. Others, including investors, lenders, and partners, may not have the same time line that you do. Be careful that you don't forfeit the dream by having someone other than yourself make the determinations as to use of capital, personnel, and time. You may never get another bite at that apple. The other side of this coin is the recognition by a business owner that growth of the business cannot be achieved without the participation of another person. Mark and Jason are the perfect examples.

The Tax Implications

Although stock participation is not always a precursor to tax problems, professional advice is available on this topic and it should never be considered a secondary issue. Keep in mind that if you sell your stock, this may be a taxable event and, in some cases, could be a staggering tax burden. This is why, in some cases, a sale of stock together with a loan might be more than just a benefit for the seller; it may also be an advantage to the investor. Watch out for this potential problem. All too often, when partners have discussions about investing in a company, the percentage factor, the control aspect, and the prerogatives and obligations of the partners have a way of obscuring the less obvious, more subtle involvements such as taxes. Don't let this become an enormous problem somewhere down the line, when it could have been addressed earlier on by some creative thinking on the part of your professionals.

Shares Are Securities

The percentage of ownership in a business is usually represented by a stock certificate that indicates the number of shares of stock that you hold in the company. Because of the number of sham deals over the years, both the states and the federal government have enacted legislation to protect the investor, the shareholder, from being bilked by unscrupulous representations. They have also instituted safeguards by which those who can't afford such investments are, in a sense, protected from themselves. Although the rationale behind these legislative protections is important, it is also important to be sure, whether you are selling or buying stock, that you have conformed to the appropriate legislation. Be sure to see your lawyer before you finalize any such purchase or sale. There are severe penalties for making a mistake!

> Always make sure you have the proper professional advice before allocating or accepting interests in a business, especially involving the purchase or sale of stock.

What Does Percentage of Ownership Mean?

The partnership concept includes a number of variables relative to investment, earnings, commissions, and the like. Don't let anyone tell you that "there's only one way." The fact of the matter is that creative thinking can set the stage for any number of alternatives in designing a partner's compensation package. The percentage of a business is referred to in many ways. Some reference the percentage by the number of shares held. Others refer to the percentage as the equity position of the investor. Always keep in mind that anything less than a majority of the equity or ownership in a business means that you don't have ultimate control of the decision making in the company.

How the Decision Makers Are Chosen

Control by the majority can be offset by giving the prerogative of decision making to certain designated officers of the company. Keep in mind that the election of officers is the job of the directors of the company, who are chosen by the shareholders. The shareholders who hold the biggest percentages of ownership have the biggest votes. This is really as simple as it gets but it is important that every partner in a partnership arrangement be aware of this sequence of operational control.

Earnings vs. Entitlements

Although it is axiomatic that distribution of profit is usually based on the percentage of ownership in a company, the compensation to partners, for various reasons, is not necessarily determined by percentage of ownership alone. Remember how Mark and Jason worked out this disparity.

Dilution

Whether you are investing in a small, closed corporation or a larger, more sophisticated company, you need to be vigilant about the shares you hold and the percentage of ownership that those shares represent. You want to make sure that subsequent investors do not undermine your percentage of ownership. For example, you may invest $10,000 for 10,000 shares of stock, which represent 10 percent of the company's ownership because there are 100,000 shares "issued and outstanding." Under some circumstances, the next investor may also acquire 10,000 shares of the company for $10,000. But if the company goes on to issue another 100,000 shares, then your 10,000 shares represent only 5 percent of the issued and outstanding shares. What the company has essentially done is leave you with the same 10,000 shares of stock, but now those 10,000 shares represent 5 percent of the issued and outstanding shares instead of 10 percent. This may not be what you had in mind, nor what the company had promised for your investment. Be sure that you understand the short- and long-term goals of the company's management team.

Right of First Refusal

Although in the big corporate arena, the public companies, you can buy and sell the shares of businesses in which you've invested, the small-business community is significantly different. When a partnership is formed, each partner is willing to make adjustments to his or her expectations because the synergy between and among the partners is the key to success. No partner, however, wants to "inherit" a stranger after another partner has died or decided to sell his or her interest to a third party. This is not what the original partnership arrangement was all about. It is for this reason that the written agreement between partners, whether it's the operating agreement in an LLC or the bylaws of a corporation, or merely the designated prerogatives and obligations in a partnership agreement, usually calls for a right of first refusal regarding all interests in the business. This means that, although the partner has a right to invite third parties to make an offer to purchase his or her stock interest, other partners may exercise their right of first refusal by acquiring that stock on exactly the same terms. They cannot negotiate for a differ-

> Make sure you value the business periodically for exit strategy as well as potential investment.

ent price or change any other aspect of the offer. They must acquire the stock on exactly the same terms as the original offer.

Increasing the Value by the Partner's Contribution

In many instances, a person may acquire a percentage interest in a business with the opportunity to acquire more of the ownership at another time. There is, however, an interesting conundrum to this opportunity. In the big companies, this opportunity allows that their next purchase will be based on the value of the company at the time the privilege is exercised. In the small-business community, this could present a problem. After all, it's the participation and contribution of each partner that increases the equity, the value of the company, at every stage. If the subsequent purchase of stock in the company is based on the growth to which the partner has contributed, then it would not be in his or her best interest to increase the value of the company by hard work. As a result, in small businesses, the partner is often granted the right to purchase an additional interest, not based on the value at the time he or she exercises this privilege but rather on the value of the company at the time he or she made the initial purchase. In this case, however hard the partner works and however great the growth of the company may be, the partner's subsequent purchase of additional shares of stock will always be at the original price. This is something for all partners to think about. Remember the story of Eleanor Spindell in Chapter 25.

Worksheet Questions

1. Why is giving up control the biggest question in examining the potential of a partnership?

2. Why is the periodic valuation of a business a critical element in a business's growth?

3. Why is it important to get professional advice relative to a stock transaction?

4. Is there more than one way to set up a partner's compensation package?

5. Is the distribution of profit the only way that a partner can get compensated?

6. When is the best time to develop an exit strategy in a partnership agreement?

7. Why is dilution an important aspect to determine at the beginning of a partnership?

8. Why is it important for the partners to have a right of first refusal?

9. Why should a partner in a small business be entitled to buy stock in the company at the same price as his or her original purchase?

CHAPTER 28

Being Creative in Building a Formula

What You Get for What You Give

Helen Grassgreen's nutritional sports bar business had been a success from the day she started it. Granted, its success in the early days was marked by minimal profit. Still, she was well received in just about every store she visited. After a short while, she had earned a positive reception in even the biggest stores in town. The product was successful, it was becoming more visible, the story of her fast-growing business was becoming a hot topic in the business community, and investors started knocking on her door.

The Business Valuation Conundrum

Although it was obvious that the business had phenomenal potential, the current profit position of the company gave it a modest value. In order to reach the next plateau of success, Helen would need a larger facility, more sophisticated equipment, and additional personnel. She knew that she would need about $400,000. The problem was that her business was really worth (aside from the potential not yet achieved) about $100,000. If she sold 10 percent of her business, based on its current valuation, she would not be able to generate the money she needed for advancing her business to the next level.

A Little Creativity

Helen, with the help of professional advice, created a scenario that tied the money she needed to the value of her business. She explained to the four investors interested in her business that she would sell 10 percent of her business to each of them provided that each loaned her company an additional $100,000. In this way, she sold them no more than 40 percent of her company, allowing her to retain 60 percent and maintain complete control. At the same time, she obtained the financing necessary to move the company forward. The investors were getting what was appropriate according to current valuation of the business and were assured that the balance of their investment would be returned. This creative scenario fell on receptive ears. Helen was on her way!

Especially Effective for Family

This basic concept of "part investment, part loan to be repaid" is often the best approach to take with family investments. There are many situations in which a member or members of a family want to help the younger generation start a business but also have a need for this same investment capital. There may be children or grandchildren whose schooling needs could be helped dramatically at some point down the road. The family fortune might be able to help one, but not the other. By separating the dollars into part investment and part loan, both situations might be accommodated. After all, the parties know that distribution of profit may be a long way down the road since reinvestment of operating profit to achieve the appropriate plateaus of success is usually the baseline for small-business growth. But if part of the money is repaid, just as a bank loan would be amortized, the family may realize a return of that portion in time to handle other family matters. The amounts to be allocated to investment and to a loan are a matter for discussion between the parties. And don't ever forget that the availability of the money is the key. Don't forget Helen's situation with the sports bars!

Is There More Than One Way to Value a Business?

Although there are many self-styled experts on the subject and many ideas relative to valuing a business, in the final analysis only one approach really counts. It is the criterion of "the business being able to buy itself." Whatever the attitude of the seller, a buyer can afford to buy a business if the operating profit of the business can do two things:

1. Enable the buyer to take care of his or her family.
2. Generate enough money to repay the purchase price of the business over a reasonable period of time.

The time frame for repayment depends, in great part, on the risk of the business and the industry of which the business is a part.

Whether you intend to take in a partner, take in an investor, sell the business, or prepare for the exiting of a partner, you will need to have a formula available for buyout purposes. The method of determining a value for the business is essential, and this chapter spells out the essentials. (For more details and explanations, see *Entrepreneur's Ultimate Guide to Buying or Selling a Business*.) Keep in mind that whether the valuation is done for the partners because of exit strategy or any other purpose, the concept of business valuation remains the same. It is the same as if the business were being sold to a third party. Again, the key is that the business must be able to buy itself.

> "A business must be able to buy itself;" this is the basic concept involved in valuations.

Mistaken Concept

Buyers usually approach the subject of a business acquisition from the standpoint of cash availability. They are sure that "cash is king." They will often

> To avoid misunderstandings, business valuations should be made periodically.

convert existing equities to cash to ensure that they have as much cash as possible. Their philosophy is that the more cash one has, the bigger the business one will be able to buy, and the more money one will be able to take from the business. Unfortunately, this bigger to bigger philosophy is entirely erroneous. There are small businesses with gross sales of $300,000, from which the owner takes a salary of $30,000. There are also businesses with gross sales of $3,000,000 from which the owner also takes a salary of $30,000. It is not necessarily the size of a business that gives owners bigger salaries; it is the way the business is operated. The real key is: What is the percentage of profit?

Sales Are Not the Indicator

This is one reason why sales or gross revenues cannot be used as methods of valuation. After all, two entrepreneurs may operate similar businesses, with one generating a profit of 10 percent and the other generating a profit of 30 percent based on the same sales picture. Which business would you want to buy? Would you pay the same for the business with 10 percent profit that you would for the business generating 30 percent profit? But the reality notwithstanding, buyers still think that the wisdom of "bigger to bigger" is sound. For this reason, after a sale the buyer's reservoir of cash has been depleted dramatically and the money to take care of the family must come from the profit of the new business. The operating profit of the business, therefore, must serve two purposes: taking care of the family and repaying the purchase price of the acquisition.

Borrowing the Money

Whether the money for a business acquisition comes from a bank, another lending source, or family and friends, or is merely the result of a buyer converting stocks, bonds, real estate, or other equity positions into cash, the money must be paid back. And don't forget that while borrowing from a lending institution may be a great idea, the reality is that this is a very unlikely scenario in most cases. Banks are notoriously interested in hard assets: brick, mortar, and dirt. They are not nearly as keen on creativity, hard work, imagination, and big dreams. In fact, in the small-business community, the greatest number of sales involve the seller taking a down payment and a promissory note for the balance of the purchase price over a specific period of time. In that case, it is quite obvious that the money must be paid because the lender is the seller.

> The bottom-line profit must serve two purposes: supporting the buyer's family and repaying the purchase price of the business.

Repaying the Purchase Price Based on Risk

Conventional wisdom together with statistics from the small-business community will tell you that sellers don't want to wait for full repayment any longer than ten years, even in the most optimistic of circumstances. And buyers want to pay for a business over the shortest possible period of time. After all, once the price has been repaid, those repayment dollars fall directly into the pocket of the new owner. Therefore, the promissory note is usually repaid within five to ten years. This time frame is based on risk. In the case of a Burger King®, for example, the general public neither knows nor cares who owns the business. As long as the quality of food, cleanliness, and service are maintained, the continuity of the business is relatively assured in good times and in bad. On the other hand, if the business is predicated on customer loyalty to an owner such as a dentist, a massage therapist, or a personal chef, the risk to continuity is substantial, and the seller will want his or her promissory note paid within the shortest possible time. Whatever the situation, it is clear that the business must generate enough profit to repay the purchase price. The operating profit of the business, therefore, must serve two purposes.

The Purpose of Your Financial Paperwork

In the normal order of business such as preparing a profit and loss statement (P&L), your financial paperwork is designed to do a number of things. The first is for you to understand the nature of the expenses necessary to generate your sales revenues. If you prepare your P&L properly, you will have a perfect setup for doing a comparative analysis, line item by line item. In this way, you will be able to reflect on those things that you might eliminate in the next year to save money. You might also note those things that are generating more sales, and those that were not so successful. The P&L serves as a chart or a road map, which should help you maintain and grow your business.

The Bottom-Line Profit

At the close of the year, your P&L will also serve to create your income tax position. As you take the appropriate deductions against your sales (revenues), you will make the operating profit (the bottom line) smaller. Because you will be paying your taxes on the basis of this bottom line, these deductions are helpful for saving on taxes. This is a good thing. On the other hand, if the bottom line is also the basis for valuing the business, this is not a good thing. The smaller the bottom line, the smaller the valuation of the business. What is the answer to this conundrum?

Reconstituting the Profit and Loss Statement

There are really two kinds of P&Ls. One is for the Internal Revenue Service (IRS), to be used for tax purposes. The other is for the selling of the business. You must keep in mind that although the government has allowed certain expenses against your sales picture to minimize the operating profit of your business for tax purposes, some of these, such as depreciation, are not cash items, and many of these deductions are not necessary for the proper operation of the business. They are advantages that the owner may enjoy but, again, are not necessary for the proper operation of the business. You must make this adjustment before making any presentation on the value of your business. There are actually three adjustments that should be made.

1. Depreciation and Amortization

The government's decision to give a "life" to an inanimate object can dramatically affect profit. The government says you can deduct the value of a car or an expensive piece of equipment but you can't deduct it all in one year. You have to deduct a percentage of it each year depending on the life of the equipment. If your new car has a cost of $30,000 and a life of five years, you can deduct $6,000, or 20 percent of the cost, annually for five years. But this is not a cash expense of the business. It is a method by which you can take this deduction, but it does not affect the cash position of the business.

> Make sure you understand how to reconstitute your P&L for valuation purposes.

Therefore, it should fall to the bottom line to indicate the real amount of cash as profit in the business.

2. Nonrecurring Expenses

What the buyer is interested in is any cost or expense for which he or she will be responsible after the sale. Nonrecurring expenses may include things such as computer software and expenses of sale preparation. Since they will not be obligations of the buyer, they can be dropped to the bottom line.

3. Expenses Personal to the Owner

These expenses are not necessary for the proper operation of the business. Such items are usually a little problematic but need to be factored in for the benefit of the valuation. The owner may be using his children to help out around the business but would not need them for the proper operation of the business. There are other prerogatives, such as business trips to trade shows on which the new buyer-owner might not want to spend the money. If these are not really necessary, they may be considered as owner's compensation and dropped to the bottom line. In this way, the IRS P&L has been converted to a "selling P&L" and the bottom line, on which the business valuation is predicated, will be bigger than the one prepared for the government's tax purposes. When making these judgments, check with your tax advisor; you should, for your own protection, get this advice as you prepare your selling scenario.

The Risk Factor

Now that you have created the basis for the business via your P&L, you must examine the risk factor in the business and in the industry to find the best bottom line. As previously noted, risk is a variable that depends on the ability of the business to survive in the face of both personal and nonpersonal circumstances that might negatively affect the business after the sale. If there is minimal risk to the business, à la Burger King®, as previously noted, the price can be higher. If the risk is fairly substantial because of the loyalty factor, customer to owner, or because of national factors that may affect revenues, or because of raw materials or component parts being vulnerable to outside influences—in other words, to a variety of things over which the owner cannot exercise control—then the risk would lower the selling price, the valuation of the business.

The Buyer Is Another Key

Although many pundits would suggest that the value of a business depends entirely on the numbers, this is definitely not the case. Remember that the bottom line must ensure that the buyer can take care of his or her family. In some cases, the buyer might require an income of $35,000 per year. Another buyer, interested in the same business, might require an annual income of $45,000 per year. If the bottom-line profit is $100,000, the seller could value the business at a greater price by selling to the buyer who only needs $35,000, because the $65,000 balance would generate a greater selling price than the $55,000 balance would allow after the $45,000 income to the other buyer. Remember, the operating profit of the business must serve two purposes: taking care of the family and repaying the purchase price of the acquisition. The lesson to be learned here is that the financial computation alone is not the end game in establishing the value of a business for sale. It is true that the reconstituted P&L, together with the risk factor, once assessed, will not change. But the character and the needs of the buyer will change with every candidate. A great deal depends on the needs of the buyer and what happens at the negotiating table. After all, it is the buyer's success on which the full payment of the promissory note to the seller depends. Don't ever forget that!

The Computation

Most partnerships, for the purpose of this examination, fall into the small-business category. The valuation, therefore, is based on the reality of the small-business experience. In this context, most small businesses are being sold with a down payment and the balance of the purchase price to be paid to the seller over a period of time. This method of payment is good reason for the seller to get a solid interest rate along with the repayment schedule, due to the risk of not being able to collect the full balance of the note. The less risk, the lengthier the promissory note, the more interest is paid, and the greater the price of the business. The greater the risk, the shorter the promissory note, the less interest is paid, and the lower the price for the business. For computation purposes, and based on the fact that the seller is accepting a risk of default on the part of the buyer, a 10 percent interest rate has been acceptable in the small-business community.

The Bottom Line Rises Again

If the bottom-line profit is $25,000, after all the expenses against revenues that are necessary for the proper operation of the business, and the risk is fairly substantial, then the business would have a valuation of $100,000. This is based on the fact that the bottom-line profit, after accounting for the money necessary for the buyer to take care of his or her family, is sufficient to pay off the $100,000 purchase price over the short (greater risk) five-year period. This $25,000 (the actual figure is $25,497) can pay off the principal of $100,000, together with the interest at 10 percent. In other words, the $25,000 is sufficient each year of the five-year payment schedule to completely amortize the promissory note during that five-year period. The payments will actually amount to $125,000 ($100,000 for the principal, and $25,000 for the interest).

If the bottom-line profit were $50,000 after accounting for the buyer's income, and the same risk prevailed, the business would be worth $200,000 because the $50,000 profit per year would be able to completely amortize $200,000 over the same five-year risk period with interest at 10 percent.

On the Other Hand

If the risk were determined to be less than the five-year risk program, say a seven-year risk program (i.e., a lesser risk), then the business with a $50,000 bottom-line profit would be worth $250,000 because the $50,000 bottom-line profit would fully amortize the $250,000 over a period of seven years at 10 percent interest. This annualized figure to pay off principal and interest each year is about $20,000 (actually $19,921).

If the business was essentially a no-risk situation, it could be worth $316,000. The $50,000 would fully amortize the $316,000 over a ten-year period at 10 percent interest. The amount for annual payments is about $15,800 (actually $15,858).

For a fuller description of business valuation and its many nuances, see *Entrepreneur's Ultimate Guide to Buying or Selling a Business.*

Although the rule of business valuation is a simple one, "The business must be able to buy itself," the devil, as always, is in the details. The above formula is a short version of the details.

Protecting the Business

The business valuation concept will give you an idea of how to establish the selling price of a business. The ultimate price can be used to establish a partner's interest for the purpose of exit strategy, as well as for buying-in. Although the concept is designed to create a set of parameters within which an appropriate price can be determined, there will be a high and a low, depending on risk, etc., as noted above. When a partner is leaving, conventional wisdom suggests that the low end of the price scale be used because the remaining partners should be entitled to the benefit of dollars and cash to maintain the continuity of the business. It is in this context that the question comes up of protecting the business. If the exit strategy is not handled appropriately, the exiting partner could be taking more money from the business than the business can actually afford. After all, most small businesses are built on the premise that any operating profit should be reinvested until the business reaches a plateau of stability and certainty. Just as a divorce proceeding should always consider the children of the marriage its highest priority, the partners, whatever their grief or agenda may be, should always consider the health of the business as their highest priority. Don't create an exit strategy for a partner that will create any vulnerability to the business.

What If My Partner Leaves?

When a partnership is formed, it is the intention of all parties that each will contribute his or her best efforts to build the business and establish a solid foundation for future growth. Despite the best of partner intentions, there are many reasons why they may not endure over the long term. Just as corporate protection against personal liability is not often usable in the early days of a business (vendors know that the business is new, and will usually require personal signatures or personal guarantees on any substantial purchase), the value of a young business is usually somewhat open to conjecture. Profit may not be realized until the business has exercised its muscle in the business marketplace for a period of time. It is difficult for a partner to leave the partnership in the early days and expect to take any substantial sum of money.

How to Create a Reality

This situation came up with Amy and Broderick when they decided to put their cosmetic business together. Although they had many conversations about goals and expectations, there was a substantial difference in their lifestyles. During the course of their discussions, questions arose relative to the possibility of one of the partners leaving: What would their interest be worth? Could they sell their interest to a third party? The conclusions they reached are interesting.

Legal Language for a New Partnership

1. In the first three (3) years of the business (from the date of incorporation), neither party will have the prerogative of selling his or her shares to any third party, and any buyout, one of the other, shall be strictly on a negotiated basis.

2. Subsequent to the third year, each shall have the right of first refusal should the other party decide to sell. However, the selling party can offer for sale to a third party no more than 49 percent interest in the company. The other 1 percent MUST be offered to the other partner, prorated to the value of the 49 percent. The

> Make sure you create a partnership agreement that will allow the remaining partner to retain control when a partner leaves the company.

purpose of this paragraph is to ensure that the remaining partner retains a controlling interest.

3. The valuation of the business at this time shall be by a valuation expert to be agreed upon by the parties or, in lieu of such agreement, by each appointing an expert, the two experts then appointing a third. Two of the three experts must then agree on a valuation of the business at that time.

An interesting side note to this story is that after less than a year, Broderick decided to leave. The language agreed to at the outset of the partnership proved to be quite valuable to Amy and to the continuity of her business.

Consideration must also be given to the business's ability to make the appropriate payments without jeopardizing the integrity of the business itself and its ability to maintain its continuity in the face of these payments.

Worksheet Questions

1. What two goals must the bottom-line profit serve in the proper valuing of a business?

2. Why is a multiple of sales or gross revenues a bad way to value a business?

3. Why does a valuation formula depend on risk?

4. What is the difference between an IRS P&L and a selling P&L?

5. Why are the buyer's needs so important in establishing the price of a business?

6. Why is price alone not the determining factor in establishing a valuation?

7. What should the value of a small business be in the early days?

CHAPTER 29

When the Judicial System Becomes Your Partner

When Protection Is Just Not Good Enough

A sweater manufacturing company, Heavenly Design (HD), noticed that several of its designs were being produced by another company. At this point, a number of questions arose. Did HD protect its designs by filing them in a timely way and with the appropriate government authority? Were the designs distinctive enough to warrant protection? The criterion was, were the copies close enough to HDs as to be "confusingly similar"? And the all-important question was, Does the manufacturing company have enough money to retain legal counsel and take the case through the grueling, time-consuming, and expensive process of litigation? It is a sobering fact that litigation is expensive, and companies must consider whether they have the funds to handle such cases all the way through. Starting a case without being able to stay the course is a very bad idea and makes you vulnerable to "the big guy" who has the money to take advantage of the system.

Smaller companies don't usually have the money to bring a legal action. The very large companies will often let the matter go because the infringement will not impact their bottom-line profit or their brand position in the marketplace. HD was a company in the middle. It had the money to proceed, and the copycat products in the marketplace were seriously injuring its brand name. Initial assessment by legal counsel was that there was, indeed, an infringement. All the preliminary correspondence was sent in the hope of prevailing upon the other side to stop the infringing activity. This proved to be of no avail. The lawsuit was started and continued for many months. As HD started to prove its claim, the appearance of the evidence during this period convinced the infringing party that the likely decision, if the case went to trial, would probably be in HD's favor. For this reason, the parties agreed to take it to mediation and it was settled—substantially in favor of HD!

The New Business Marketplace

The proliferation of small businesses in the past 50 years and the business aspects of e-commerce in more recent days are leading to a substantial increase in civil litigation. The issue of using someone's product name or business or product concept has been getting a good deal of attention. One aspect of this is the employee who violates the terms of his or her noncompetition contract clause by taking confidential information or customer lists to his or her new employer. This is essentially stealing. The problem of enforcement is quite another issue. See your legal professional whenever this appears on your business horizon.

The problem of the internet and its sharing of information worldwide, especially the concept of appropriating the materials and products of others, has opened a whole new spectrum of legal activity. Some software has even been developed that allows the sharing of information anonymously. Most experts agree that trying to protect against such an intrusion by encrypting the information and making it available only to those with the decoding device is not likely to afford long-term protection.

The Nondisclosure and Copyright

Many entrepreneurs with ideas and even those with working models are approaching large companies in the hope that they will either be funded or acquired. Before making any disclosure about their product or idea, they have usually been advised by counsel to have the company sign a nondisclosure agreement to keep the information confidential. Some companies don't even want to see the product or concept for fear that they will be facing a lawsuit if they bring a similar product to market that they may have been working on for years internally. On the other hand, this information may be just what they've been looking for to complete a project that needed this kind of tweaking. In this case, the entrepreneur may well have a case against the company.

> Don't get involved in a lawsuit unless you're sure that you can carry the burden of this litigation all the way through to the end.

Date of First Use

What about songwriters or authors who see their product taken by others? This is what copyrighting is all about. The date of first use will usually prevail unless it can be shown that it was actually misappropriated, with the intent to profit at the expense of the original author.

The Quicker Fixer

In addition to contract or tort cases, there is an interesting remedy available to people whose rights are being violated on a continuing basis. The remedy is for the court to say, "Stop!" This can be done by going to the equity side of the court where a judge will recognize the potential damage involved in allowing the encroachment to continue. After all, it could take, optimistically, two to three years to finalize a case in court. By the time the case is over, the damage is irreparable, and no amount of money can adequately compensate the party whose rights were violated. A judge, on the equity side, can stop the

> Understand the limited protection afforded by noncompete and nondisclosure agreements.

infringing conduct until the matter is completely resolved. You can see that this is a delicate balance and a judge must decide which of the alternative solutions will be best for the parties. In some cases, the court might allow the infringement to continue with certain monies being held in escrow pending the decision of the parties' rights. In other cases, the court may decide that the best approach is to maintain the status quo until the matter can be heard and resolved. Be sure to consult with a legal professional if this remedy appears to be appropriate in your case.

Then There's the Tort Case

It's bad enough when doctors talk about myocardial infarction, although fortunately the number of times we need to respond is limited. But when lawyers start talking about tortious misconduct, it's time for a little clarity. In business, the subject can and will come up frequently. It's something that all partners should be aware of.

Civil vs. Criminal Misconduct

First of all, let's set the record straight. A myocardial infarction is simply a heart attack. And tortious misconduct merely refers to an interference with someone's rights. There are intentional torts—an assault on someone's person that would certainly qualify as an interference. This infringement on a person's rights could also qualify as a criminal offense subject to punishment by the state. Most torts you will run across are not so dramatic and would likely be subject to compensation in the civil, not the criminal, courts. But not always.

You may be the owner of real estate and have someone trespass on your property. This means that someone has intentionally, without the appropriate authority, entered your private space. Certainly, this is an intentional tort, an infringement on your rights. However, unlike the situation in which the party enters your property in a fast-moving car with the intention of creating serious damage or injury, this infraction would not likely be addressed in the criminal courts.

It is interesting that many such torts could be reported to the authorities for criminal action in addition to a civil suit for compensation. Most government authorities, however, refuse to participate in what they refer to as "civil matters," where the practical solution is money rather than jail. You've got to consider this before you jump to the conclusion that anything is a criminal matter. The best example is a fraudulent application by which the applicant gets money. The police consider this a civil matter and will not usually get involved. The exceptions, of course, are cases of the elderly being defrauded in a scheme. Even in domestic-violence cases, the authorities would prefer to leave the matter to the civil side rather than consider an indictment on the criminal side.

> Remember that an equity court can be a temporary but immediate resolution to certain legal problems.

The Negligence Factor

What about the person who slips and falls on your steps because you've neglected to prepare them properly for access? You could be guilty of tortious misconduct. You will be accused of having been negligent in your responsibilities. The interesting aspect to this tort is the fact that your responsibility, your level of negligence, changes depending on the status of the person injured. That is, was the injured person invited to enter the property, implied as in the case of a mailperson, or explicit as in the case of a guest? Was the person soliciting without an invitation, implied or otherwise? Was the person a trespasser, in which case your level of responsibility might be minimal?

Contracts and Torts

Although it is not entirely correct in all jurisdictions (and there are exceptions), a good reference for the layperson is to recognize that lawsuits fall, basically, into two categories: contracts and torts. If you end up in a lawsuit, as either a plaintiff or a defendant, and it is not a matter of contract, it will likely be a tort case. A contract usually defines the obligations and prerogatives of both parties. The tort usually is the result of basic standards of prerogatives and responsibilities that the law has set over time. The purpose is to establish and ensure a rational relationship between and among people during their normal interactive business and personal activities.

An auto accident will result in a tort case in that each party will seek to show that the other was at fault. This fault will be assessed based on established rules of the road. What about the driver who is under the influence of alcohol or drugs? What about the driver who is uninsured? What about the driver without a license? How do you think each of these circumstances might affect the outcome of a lawsuit? Do you think that the local legislation will have any effect on the outcome of these situations?

Intentional and Unintentional

Convincing someone to part with money or other valuables by virtue of deceit or misrepresentation will also, if proven, constitute a tort. Having harmful substances in food products, although certainly not intentional, will constitute an infringement on the rights of the consumer. A legal action, "sounding in tort" (the expression often used by the legal community), would be initiated. Any ensuing illness or injury would be the reason for the lawsuit. To win, one would need to prove that the unanticipated substance was the cause of the illness or injury. But note a big difference: a chicken bone in chicken soup might not win, whereas a piece of glass probably would. The chicken bone might be somewhat anticipated—the piece of glass, not. In another business context, negligence is represented by equipment that fails to perform consistently with its purpose or design; e.g., an automobile repair that is done badly and causes an accident.

The Tort Case

Many will seek reparation in the courts because they feel offended that their rights were not respected. They feel they are entitled to satisfaction. The tort case, however, is composed of two basic elements: negligence and damages. Without being able to show both, you will not likely prevail against the offending party. A simple example may be found in the automobile accident. The other party may have been totally responsible, but you might not have incurred any damage or injury. On the other hand, you might have sustained severe damage or injury, but the court might decide that the other person was not really to blame. In either case, you would not prevail. After all, in the middle of winter, with ice and snow on the road, many accidents have happened without anyone being responsible in a negligent way. And

> Remember that you need both liability and damages if you expect to prevail in a lawsuit.

even though you may have incurred injuries or damage to your vehicle, there might not be anyone to sue. Consider other situations in which there are damages without anyone being held responsible. What about an act of God?

What about the Secondary Responsibility?

When a customer in a print shop seeks to copy a work that is not his or her own, and the printer makes the copies that the customer sells for profit, where is the responsibility when the printer makes no money from the deception? The answer is to avoid the problem by having the correct form filled out by the customer by which he or she shows permission to copy and use, or that the law allows copying on an isolated basis for educational purposes, etc. On the other hand, problems often slip through the cracks, and lawsuits are not unusual in such circumstances. The positive side of this, however, is that the law doesn't usually punish or try to assess blame on those who were innocent victims of the deceit. Best, however, to be careful to protect against the problem rather than to depend on the discretion of the court, or your ability to prove that you were, in fact, an innocent victim.

The Last Protection

Although careful thought and good judgment will often be the best protection, no one is so careful as to avoid all incidents. After all, the careful driver can be involved in an accident through no fault of his or her own. And the person who intends to defraud, deceive, or manipulate usually has given the matter a great deal of thought and prior planning. The victim is often a person who feels that most people are honest. The typical victim, therefore, does not usually anticipate and plan against deception and is vulnerable to those with larceny in their hearts. Whether the tort is intentional or unintentional, vulnerability is obvious.

You should respect the rights and privileges of others while expecting them to pay the same attention to yours. If you think yours have been stepped on, see your legal professional.

Worksheet Questions

1. Do you know the difference between civil and criminal misconduct?

2. Do you understand the difference between a contract action and a tort action?

3. Do you think that a nondisclosure form will protect your confidential information?

4. Do you know what kinds of matters an equity court is designed to handle?

5. Do you think that timely filing with the appropriate government agency will protect against people who want to infringe on your copyrights?

6. Do you understand how long it takes and how expensive it is to bring a lawsuit for infringement?

7. Do you think that "date of first use" is important in a copyright infringement case?

Glossary

Accelerated growth. The growing of a business within an extraordinarily short time frame.

Accounts payable. Money owed by a business for the purchase of goods or services.

Accounts receivable. Money owed to a business for the purchase of goods or services.

Accrual accounting. The method by which revenues and expenses are computed as incurred, even though payment has not been received.

Advisor. A person who acts in an advisory capacity to a business.

Agent. A person or business that has the authority to act on someone else's behalf.

Amortization. The method by which a "soft" asset (e.g., a franchise) can be expensed over a period of time based on a fictional "asset life."

Angel investor. A person who invests in a company with expectations of a return of a multiple of his or her investment.

Balance sheet. A picture of the assets, liabilities, ratios, and equity of a business at any given moment in time. Comparing one balance sheet with another will show activity and change in a business.

Break even. The point at which operating income is neither a profit nor a loss.

Business model. A particular method of operating a business for profit.

Business plan. A written analysis of a business, its state of affairs, and its road map to the future.

Business valuation. The value of the earned equity in a business at any moment in time.

Cadre. The internal group of people making up the operational capability of a business.

Cash accounting. The method by which revenues and expenses are computed only when payment is received or paid for goods and services.

Cash flow. The flow of dollars into and from a business for goods or services purchased or sold.

Clone. A potential business buyer who already owns a business similar in most respects to the seller's.

Collateral. Assets used as security.

Competition. Other businesses of like kind with which you share your potential customer base.

Competitive analysis. An exposition of the values of your product or service relative to the competition in the marketplace.

Confidentiality agreement. A written agreement that prevents all signatories from disclosing proprietary information. Also referred to as a nondisclosure agreement.

Confidential information. Information that should not be shared with anyone other than the designated people in a business.

Consultant. A person whose experience in business allows him or her to act as a business advisor.

Copyright. A method of protecting proprietary information by determining date of first use.

Corporation. A legal entity that protects investors from any liability or loss beyond the original investment.

Cost of sales (product). The cost of goods or components or raw material necessary to produce or have products or services available for sale.

Depreciation. A method by which capital investments are deducted from revenues over a fixed period of years for tax purposes.

Dilution. The issuance of additional shares of stock in a corporation to a new investor that changes the original investor's percentage of participation.

Disclosures. UFOC, Uniform Franchise Offering Circular, Federal Disclosure Document. A full disclosure required to sell a franchise in all 50 states.

Directors and officers liability insurance (D&O policy). To insulate members of a board of directors against lawsuits directed against them as individuals.

Equity. (a) The amount of ownership in a company. (b) A court that hears matters that need an immediate or interim decision.

Escrow. A place where dollars or other valuable assets can be held pending the conclusion of anticipated action by the parties.

Executive summary. The first page or so of a business plan that acts as a précis to the plan itself.

Exit strategy. The method by which a partner or investor is expected to be compensated when exiting a business venture.

Expenses against revenues. The concept of costs against sales leading to profit.

Feasibility study. A document that examines whether a business has the potential for success in the marketplace.

Fiduciary. A person or other entity entrusted with the responsibility to protect the goods or monies of someone who has created the relationship.

Financial assumptions. Narrative explanations that clarify the numbers in a financial document.

Franchise. A method of replicating a business that involves the investment and participation of an individual owner and fees or royalties to the originator for use of the business name and marketing concept.

Golden parachute. The reservoir of dollars and retirement benefits offered to an executive on termination or retirement.

Growth by acquisition. The growing of a business by acquiring other businesses in the same or a related trade or industry.

Guru. A person whose credentials suggest that they know all about a particular issue.

Horizontal growth. The acquisition of a similar business for expansion.

Income statement. (See profit and loss statement.)

Incremental growth. The growing of a business by small but constant moves from one plateau of success to another.

Inevitable disclosure. The concept of an individual utilizing what he or she has learned by virtue of their involvement in a particular trade or industry.

Inhouse capability. The ability of a business to handle operating elements by using equipment and personnel inside the parameters of the company.

Indictment. The legal term indicating that the state is putting a person on trial for an illegal act.

Initial Public Offering (IPO). The creation of an opportunity for stock participation in the equity of a company by outsiders.

IRS P&L. The income statement prepared for tax purposes. Compare with the reconstituted P&L.

Joint venture. A partnership relationship between two companies to take advantage of their synergy.

Key man insurance. Insurance policy to pay for the demise of a partner in a business.

Limited partnership. A legal entity with total responsibility in the general partner.

Matrix. A vertical and horizontal chart that creates a comparative analysis of the products, values, and prices of competition in the marketplace.

Merger. The coming together of two business entities.

Negligence. The failure of a person to act properly and in accordance with reasonable caution.

Niche position. A place in the competitive marketplace that makes a business unique.

Nondisclosure agreement. A written agreement that prevents all signatories from disclosing proprietary information. Also referred to as a confidentiality agreement.

Outsourcing. The use of other businesses to handle certain aspects of your business operation.

Partnership. A legal entity between two or more individuals or businesses participating in business for profit. Also, in the generic sense, any relationship between two or more people or entities for business purposes.

Patent. The method by which a concept product can be protected against the unfair use by others.

Phantom partnership. A relationship created to give comfort and assurance to clients during a transition period as part of the sale of a business.

Profit and loss statement (P&L). A financial statement, usually done on an accrual basis, designed to show a picture of the business's expenses against sales.

Protocol. The method by which operations are best handled in a business.

Purchase money promissory note (PMPN). The promissory note that represents the balance of a purchase price after a down payment is made.

Receivable turnover period. The time frame between the sale of goods and receipt of payment.

Reconstituting the P&L. A method by which only those expenses against revenues that are necessary for the proper operation of a business for sale are depicted.

Return of investment. The money returned to an investor.

Return on investment. The "bonus" returned to an investor for the use of his or her money.

Right of first refusal. The right of an owner to acquire another owner's stock position instead of allowing an outside third party to do so.

Status quo. The state of affairs that a court decides not to change until all the facts are examined in a legal dispute.

Strategic alliance. The working together of two or more legal entities to enjoy the synergy they can create.

Synergy. The phenomenon of two entities working together being more productive than the aggregate of the two entities working separately.

Trade secrets. The proprietary information about a business or product or service of a business.

Tort. The interference with someone's right to privacy, property, or well-being.

Tortious misconduct. The activity by a person that creates a tort against another person or his or her property.

Trespass. The act of somebody intruding on the person or space of another.

Vertical growth. Growing your company by generating an inhouse capability for the acquisition of component parts or raw materials necessary to create your product or the establishment of a distribution outlet for selling your manufactured product.

Working capital reservoir. The money available to a business for operating expenses and contingencies.

About the Author

Ira N. Nottonson is a Law Review Graduate of Boston College Law School and is licensed to practice law in the Commonwealth of Massachusetts and the State of California. He has practiced general litigation and business/franchise law with partnerships in Boston, Massachusetts, and Westwood, California. At present, he confines his consulting practice to business valuations and the needs of the small business community.

Mr. Nottonson has acted in various capacities for many companies, both private and public: chief executive officer, chief operating officer, and chief legal counsel. He has also, at various times, been responsible for marketing and franchise sales, and has acted as consultant for hundreds of companies throughout the United States and the United Kingdom. These companies include International House of Pancakes, Orange Julius of America, House of Pies, PIP Printing, PIP/UK (the British subsidiary of PIP Printing), Quickprint of America (the Big Red Q Quickprint Centers), Copper Penny Family Restaurants, The Bryman-Sawyer Schools, and United Rent-All.

In his legal capacity, Mr. Nottonson has served as a member of the management committees for all of the above companies. He has been an integral part of the planning and implementation of basic business concepts.

Mr. Nottonson's qualifications are particularly unique as he has also been an entrepreneur in his own right. He has been the owner of an advertising agency, a television production company, a publishing company, a law practice, and a nightclub. This diverse background has given him a better understanding of the day-to-day problems of business from a very personal perspective.

Mr. Nottonson currently works with both start-ups and challenging situations needing negotiation and reconstruction. He has been appointed as arbiter by the court and has testified on the subjects of small business and business valuations. He has written extensively on the general subject of business for various newspapers and periodicals and writes a monthly business column for the *Boulder Daily Camera* in his hometown of Boulder, Colorado. In addition, he has been guest lecturer at various colleges and universities, as well as a lecturer at the Chamber of Commerce in Boulder under the auspices of the Small Business Development Center. An articulate exponent of business concepts, he has also appeared over the years on radio and television.

Mr. Nottonson is author of *Entrepreneur's Ultimate Guide to Buying or Selling a Business* and *Before You Go into Business, Read This!*

Index